INTERNATIONAL MUSIC COUNCIL

2

ALAIN DANIELOU
in collaboration with
JACQUES BRUNET

THE SITUATION OF MUSIC
AND MUSICIANS
IN COUNTRIES OF THE ORIENT

Translated by JOHN EVARTS

LEO S. OLSCHKI - FLORENCE
MCMLXXI

FIRST PUBLISHED IN JUNE 1971 AS VOLUME TWO IN THE
SERIES « MUSIC AND COMMUNICATION ». COMMISSIONED BY
THE INTERNATIONAL MUSIC COUNCIL UNDER A GRANT FROM
THE CALOUSTE GULBENKIAN FOUNDATION

———

EDITION LIMITED TO 2000 COPIES

———

INTRODUCTION

CRAFTSMANSHIP AND INDUSTRY

The problems which face the art of music in the countries of Asia and Africa today are of a general order – problems which have grown out of the uncontrolled development of an industrial society in which no precautions were taken to protect the culture, the crafts and the arts. The latter have tended to become mere consumers' products, independent of the social context. The freedom of expression, which was the source of their constant renewal, no longer exists.

In the field of the arts, a fundamental conflict has appeared between the metier of an artisan and industrial art. Painting has generally been able to remain an individual art – a metier, even though it is open to commercial pressures. The theatre, too, remains a metier, but must compete commercially with films and television.

Music, on the other hand, tends to become essentially an industrial product, the result of the work of several individuals, to fabricate a finished product which can be exploited through wide commercial circulation. In such a situation, the direct expression of living creativity, whether individual or collective, has difficulty in finding its place. Within what setting today would Chopin improvise his preludes? Before what public, today saturated by the radio and television, could the great African or Asian artist

— 1 —

create a work according to his mood of the moment? Concerts tend to become presentations of stars who are known through the records they have made, whereas the record should only be a reminder of the concert. Of the living music in which improvisation plays an essential part, a gramophone record gives us only a frozen on fixed moment, like a photograph of a dancer, and it is this fixed form which tends to appear as a norm.

All societies, under one form or another, are divided into four groups or castes: intellectuals, soldiers, farmers-business-men, and craftsmenworkmen. In small societies, these functions can be successive or concomitant for individuals. Their categories are inevitably professional. The princes and kings belong to the soldier caste, and in difficult periods, almost everywhere, even among peoples who believe themselves freed from castes, it is the army that takes over the power.

Every human grouping, whether at the scale of a tribe, a village, a province or a state, produces the essential elements of culture, of justice, of the arts. The most isolated tribe possesses its literature (oral), its stories, its poets, its musicians, its painters and artisans who are technically professionals, even if they concurrently practise another metier. Spectacles – dance and theatre – generally require a more numerous public which may be formed jointly by a certain number of villages, so that the time of preparation which a performance requires can be economically supported by the community.

Almost all the village communities in Asia have their traditions of theatrical performances, in which music plays an essential role, often at a very refined level. Many members of the community take part in these performances.

An important part of the life of all the communities – today we would call it their « leisure time » – is set aside for cultural activities, whether it's a question of the story-teller, who is the living depository of the group's

A copy of this book « The Situation of Music and Musicians in Countries of the Orient » by Alain Daniélou, one of a series of three published by the International Music Council (UNESCO) under the general title of « Music and Communication », is being sent free to all subscribers to « The World of Music ». The publication of the book has been made possible through the generosity of the Calouste Gulbenkian Foundation.

history and who narrates and sings its heroic or dramatic events in the course of winter evenings, or of the musicians, who are indispensable for all celebrations, ceremonies, marriages or funerals, or of groups of dancers and actors, who, during the off-season period for farming and hunting, present the legends of heroes and gods and the loves and dramas of men.

These artists are necessarily specialists, professionals, chosen for their aptitudes; through long effort and training, they achieve a degres of technique which easily equals that acquired in the Conservatories of the big cities. The idea that « folklore » artists are not professionals comes from a misunderstanding of the meaning of the word – a word which originated in a society where popular or folk art was systematically destroyed.

Multiplied by a vast number of different groups, in countries which are profoundly different in their origins, their tendencies and their histories, it is these craftsmen who have established the bases of all the arts; they are, in fact, the depositories of the arts and the inexhaustible source of all artistic tradition.

The drummer of an Indian village is in no way technically inferior to the most celebrated concert musicians.

And it is from such drummers, for example, that our best jazz drummers discover that they have much to learn. Village theatre troupes, such as those of the Kathâkali, reach an astonishing technical perfection. The same is true of the orchestras and dancers of Bali, of the shadow-theatre groups of Cambodia, Malaysia and Thailand, and of the « popular » theatres of Viet Nam. Their level of achievement makes it impossible to consider them as less sophisticated than the orchestras or troupes of the palaces or large cities. It is the same everywhere; in spite of the prejudices which obstruct them as a consequence of the cultural colonialism of the urban centres. Even in the Occident, a good Flamenco dancer, a great Gypsy violinist, a tar-player from Azerbaidjan, are in fact, technically and artistically, artists of the very highest order. From where, then, one is led to ask, do we get this paternalistic notion of « folklore » and the systematic destruction of this artistic life of peoples, the right which the « amateurs » of the cities take upon themselves to arrange, to « organise » art forms about which they understand nothing? The « folklore groups » are striking examples of noble art forms which have been soiled and degraded by the arrangements of city folk. The romantic notion which tries to convince us of the existence of a spontaneous and naive folklore — implying that everything which is not the bourgeois art of the cities is necessarily primitive — is the consequence of a cultural colonialism growing from the industrialisation of urban centres, from the fabrication of standardized products, from canned products, which the commercial powers seek to substitute for the products of the craftsman's art.

What would the wine merchants do if, in spite of artful devices and chemical products, the « grands crus » did not always have the same taste? And what would the concert impresarios do if the duration and form of a concert were different each time, and if the public were a bit lost due to the absence of over-familiar themes? This is why the industrial society tends to favor a standardized, and consequently saleable, artistic product. The art of a craftsman, which forms a part of life and of musical and theatrical creation in which the population takes part, permits the artist to earn his living but it is not a commercial product.

The origin of musical standardization which has made it possible for music to be made an article of commerce was notation, and, especially, printing. It isn't that notation in itself is not useful as an aide-memoire. In one form or another, it has always existed everywhere. But the substitution of the printed product for the oral tradition

— 4 —

and for its artistic performances caused the first de-perso-nalisation of creative communities. It gave birth to an unbelievable superiority complex in the notator – actually ignorant in comparison to the unlettered but cultured artist. Musical notation, which tends to reduce the music to what can be written, has limited and distorted the very conception of the art of music in the countries which prac- tise it. It has separated the composer from the interpreter and performer, and everywhere where it serves as the basis for performance, it has led music towards an impasse – from which, incidentally, it seeks a way out today – and, in any case, has caused people to reject, ignore or treat as inferior some of the most subtle forms of music which go beyond the limits of the possibilities of notation. And this is the case for all the musical cultures of Asia and Africa.

The ancient conceptions of music which have succeeded in surviving and which, in fact, have an affinity with the most modern, are those which have ignored or refused notation and which, for this reason alone, we too easily call folklore, whether it is Gypsy art or Flamenco, great Indian music or Iranian or Arab. What would remain of the rhythm of a jazz drummer if he had to read from a score? In the same way, there would remain nothing of the subtle attacks, the ornaments, the nuances of intervals which form the essential core of the meaning of modal music. An apt parallel would be the difference between a speaker who reads his text and one who speaks spon- taneously – who improvises.

After notation, there came records, the radio and television, all tending to substitute imported, pre-fabricated products for the local musical artistry. By the very perfec- tion of its manufacture, industrial art discourages the ar- tisan's art, though in fact it does not possess the fine qua- lities of the latter.

When the public ceases to participate in artistic crea- tion, it loses interest in it, since the art no longer forms a part of the public's emotional life. The cult of the star performer replaces the appreciation of the work of art, the listeners judge according to modish criteria and snobbishness, the manufactured product served up to them, but which always remains foreign to them for they know nothing about the techniques of its invention.

Whether we consider orchestra conductors or chansonniers, it is saddening to see that the same furious enthusiasm is shown for their worst and most inexcusable productions as for their best. This is never so in the case of the art of the craftsman where the public consists of connoisseurs who can perceive the finest nuances of interpretation and who encourage the musician for his inventiveness, for his good performance – for they could, with a little extra work, play in his place.

The problem of the great musical traditions is a general problem. It is linked to the conflict between the crafts and industry, between a metier and mass production. No one would seriously think of rejecting all industrial products, as Gandhi wished to do, but for music, as is already the case for other forms of craftsmanship, the order of values must be reversed. In an industrial society, the craft product is a luxury product which should be protected and encouraged. We recognise this as far as textiles are concerned – and shoes and furniture and foods. But we still have a long way to go to make people realise that what is important for music is that what is most precious should be paid the highest price. It is not the orchestra groups which repeat and maltreat the same works indefinitely, but rather the player of the Indian *sitar*, the Iranian singer, the player of the Arabian *ud* – living and delicate flowers whose fugitive and always renewed creativity is the very essence of music – which no pre-fabbricated music can ever replace. It is at *their* service that the technical media should be put. It is to *them* that the place of honour in our concert halls should be given.

Only if we do this shall we be able to safeguard for the future the prestigious heritage of the various musical cultures, including our own, for without the contribution of the living and infinitely diversified creativity of the craftmusicians – of their music – musical industrialisation will lead us inevitably to the paralysis of an art become universally banal and incapable of revivifying itself alone. The necessity of a return towards an artisan-art can be observed today in the West in the numerous small jazz or pop groups.

In the West itself, today there is no longer in « serious » music any German, Italian, Spanish or French music but a global, experimental, strictly international and abstract art. The depersonalisation, growing from a desire for commercial distribution, ends up by reacting against the very centre from which it originated. It is thus that empires lose their vitality and destroy themselves – as a result of their own expansion. Music, linked originally to language, to the expression of emotions and the feelings of human beings, and which has, because of this, –like language – developed very varied and complex idioms which made for increasingly subtle and profound forms of expression, suddenly finds itself deprived of its principal role and removed from this original purpose.

The new sound structure represents a new art which has little in common with what we used to call music.

Concrete or electronic music, despite its vaguely scientific pretensions, seems to withdraw completely today from the audio-mental phenomena upon which musical languages were always based. It aims at something quite different from that which was at the origin of the development of musical idioms.

The broadening of international horizons makes us realise that the monuments of Angkor or the temples of Egypt are as important for us, for our history, for our aesthetic, as the Gothic cathedrals. Broadening of culture should lead us to enrichment. For music, it seems to be nothing more than the tendency to reduce it to a common denominator. We live in an epoch of political nationalism and cultural de-nationalisation. We can, nevertheless, observe that it is only psychological and social factors which are at work in Asia to substitute a universal and impersonal music – though with its own signature – for the national or regional forms of the musical art which, though often created anonymously, are profoundly personal in character and in the way they are produced. If we wish to avoid losing the precious heritage, the immense variety of sound techniques which the countries of the Orient have preserved for us, we must approach them with respect and reconsider our methods. For, the difficulties of explaining the structures and content of the musical languages of the Orient with the use of the terminology of European musicology, the nonsense resulting from the various systems of notation which have been used, and which are as inadequate for the essentially fluid musical forms as the systems which people have attempted to create to notate dance movements, the imprecision caused by the introduction of Western solfege in notating the music of the Orient –all of this has only brought about a general misunderstanding and disastrous results. This fact should lead us to revise our methods and to study the diverse forms of musical language, beginning with its interior essence, with the meaning of the music and not with arbitrary « facts » defined in terms of a musicological science which is interested only in the external aspects as seen through the perspective of a particular culture.

I

THE CONFLICT BETWEEN
THE ORIENT AND THE OCCIDENT

BACKGROUND

To arrive at a genuine understanding of the diverse musical traditions, of the diverse musical languages, it seems essential first of all to have a thorough knowledge and inclusive view of the cultures to which the different conceptions of the art of music belong and of the principles upon which they are based; and, thereafter, to approach analytically the structural elements of musical languages leaving aside all acquired notions, all scales of values, all the prejudices and defenses which our own tradition unconsciously inflicts upon us.

If we examine history from the moment that the Orient and Occident – a relatively recent period – began to reestablish contacts which had existed in antiquity, and to become aware of each other, we find that these first contacts were more often in the form of antagonisms, never or very rarely, when faced with each other's culture, expressed in the form of reciprocal understanding. Whether it was a question of religion (the Crusades, missions), of politics (conquests), or of social schemes (colonisation), the meeting of the two civilisations was usually characterised *not* by an attempt at co-existence, but rather by an opposition and a systematic endeavor on the part of the stronger to impose its culture, its religion, its language upon the « less privileged » group; and one finds little evidence that any sincere effort was made to evaluate what the conquering people sought to destroy – those elements for which they wished to substitute their own way of life and their own beliefs.

The musical culture of the Orient – like all the other non-European cultures – has had to submit to « contacts » which were established in the course of past centuries with the Occident. Obviously, the oppression of one culture by another fragments and devalues traditional concepts, tending to deform them if not to cause them to disappear completely. The few human islands which have survived the massive invasions have been able, in rare cases, to retain their customs and their language, but more often these groups have been forced to accept the changes in the social order which brought about serious upheavals in their traditions and their culture. Examples are numerous where Shaman ceremonies, forbidden for would-be humanitarian reasons which were opposed to sacrifice, forbade as a consequence the bewitching music which accompanied the ceremony. It is still not uncommon today in certain Asian countries which are strongly influenced by Western ideas that certain celebrations, which seem immoral to the foreigner, are forbidden. This is an evolution, it seems, which modern life makes inevitable in a world which, while pretending to become better, eliminates elements favouring stability and the canalization of human instincts, and ends up with exactly opposite results. Sometimes, however, the contacts between two cultures have brought about new artistic fermentation; this was the case of the Greek kingdoms in North-west India, which engendered the flowering of Greco-Buddhist art.

In the same way, the « silk route » was the original cause of the expansion and growth of the great Hindu cultures of Southeast Asia, where local cultures assimilated certain aspects of the Hindu civilisation to create, in their turn, entirely original civilisations. But these cases were real exchanges and not cultural colonialism.

From the beginning of the Christian Era to the end of the Middle Ages, the points of contact between Occident and Orient were numerous. The Greek kingdoms in Northern India survived for a long period. The Mongolian Empire extended as far as Budapest; the Arabs occupied Spain and the Turks, Byzantium. The Troubadours crossed the frontiers of civilisations and the Tziganes brought in elements of Indian and Iranian music throughout the Occident. Thus, their contribution is no less important than that of African musical art to jazz and to contemporary music as a whole. After the Mongolian invasions, the birth of Gothic art, which follows closely the decline of Hindu religious art and which resembles the latter in surprising ways, has not yet been clarified.

When the members of the Camerata in Florence, wishing to re-establish the theatre of antiquity, set up the basic principles of modern opera, their efforts resulted in the creation of formal structures which strongly resembled the conceptions of this theatre of antiquity which the Tazie represents: heroic drama sung — such as still exists in Iran today.

It was shortly before the period of Monteverdi that the gates between the cultures closed, and the rediscovery of the Orient thereafter became sporadic and fragmentary — despite the increasingly frequent contacts.

COLONIZATION

The most important event to influence the relations between the musical traditions of the Orient and the Occident, as well as the development of music within Asia and Africa, was colonization. which set off psychological

— 11 —

and social shocks from which those countries upon which it was imposed are still far from having recovered.

Abruptly, all the traditions, all ideas of art and aesthetics, as well as moral values and religious beliefs, – all were placed in question, the elements of balance in life were cut off, and a material and false spiritual invasion caused an upheaval of everything concerned with social structures as well as beliefs and the arts. The effect was like that of a hurricane sweeping down on the cultures, and the consequences can still be felt; this period of history annihilated artistic drives and removed from the universal patrimony an incalculable number of musical masterpieces.

It was a veritable disaster for the non-European cultures in the sense that the unjustified conviction that the peoples of the West brought the benefits of a superior culture to other, less-developed peoples served as an excuse for the destruction of the very values which composed the originality of the non-Occidental civilisations. In the same way that technical devices, introduced by the Occident, were in principle considered as superior, so, too, the facile aspects of Western music, introduced into Asian countries, immediately enabled the least gifted musicians to ignore the difficult techniques, the problems of inspiration and improvisation and the long training necessary for most performers of the music of countries of the Orient, and to pass themselves off as being in the avant-garde of progress. The by-products of music of the Occident became particulary evident among the least erudite circles of the population due to the facility with which these elements could be absorbed and retained.

Furthermore, the peoples of Asia, submerged by the technical and material contributions of a civilisation which considered itself superior in everything and refused « a priori » even to study the indigenous techniques, did everything they could to imitate what the Occident had brought them. This resulted in a serious psychological crisis – in a depersonalisation wich is apparent in all the forms of contemporary art.

The crisis in Asia is revealed in the costly efforts not to be different from the Occident – the pole of attraction towards which all the desires for modernisation converge. This is historically linked up with the political, economic and industrial domination of Europe, and later, of the United States, and through this domination, they have concomitantly imposed their cultural and technical imperialism.

The forced adoption of a culture, of a language, of a religion or of strange customs, amounts to a collective brainwashing and cultural genocide. At first, this may appear to be an advantage, when the adopted culture seems to be more highly developed, more « advanced » than the original culture of the people receiving it. It requires centuries, however, for such a change of personalities to be sufficiently assimilated, to enable the peoples thus brutalized in their most inner nature to contribute anything original or anything of real value to world culture in general. This view can easily be explained since we know today that aptitudes or characteristics acquired by an ethnic group bring about, in the long run, genetic changes and become a part of the collective personality which makes possible the flourishing of a given civilisation. A change of culture, it is clear, inevitably creates at first a state of inferiority; the results of this change will continue to be imitative and never really creative. This is very different from a broadening of culture through the study of foreign languages and civilisations, once the basic education of a child has been provided within the context of his own culture.

Children who have acquired a perfect mastery of the language of their parents and have thereafter studied a foreign language of a very different structure, know how to use this language at quite a different level than if they had studied it as their principal language from their earliest years. One should not forget that in many fields – even scientific and technical fields – certain countries of the Orient had developed to a stage more highly advanced than Europe at the time of the colonial invasions. In medicine, in mathematics, in naval architecture etc., the Hindus were much more « modern » than the Europeans of the 18th Century. These sciences and techniques, however, were ignored and scorned, and their development paralyzed.

Whatever may have been the self-styler benefits which they pretended to bring to the « under-developed » peoples whom they conquered, the colonial empires actually had no aim higher than to obtain cheap labour and advantageous markets, while systematically lowering the standard of living, and, consequently, retarding the technical development of the colonialised peoples. Whenever the profit extracted from the population was deemed insufficient, genocide and expropriation were practised and still are, as in the case of the American Indians, certain regions of Africa, and the original populations of Australia.

The colonists, in such cases, were simply continuing the practise of the great invaders of Europe's proto-historical period. The notion of « under-development », so much *a la mode* today, is linked to the idea of the standard of living, which is always extremely relative and which has nothing to do with culture. One can live in great comfort and luxury, surrounded by the most cultivated arts, –without bank-notes, plumbing or frigidaires, and with none of the means which seem essential for a minimum of comfort to the European petit-bourgeois. The comment of the famous educator, Madame Montessori, when she visited India: « *Che poverta, non hanno neanche scarpe!* » in a country whose climate makes the wearing of shoes not only useless but a veritable torture, is characteristic of a fundamental misunderstanding. And it is in such matters that the aid the « under-developed » countries in sometimes incredibly absurd – even if we overlook the case of the U.S.S.R. sending snow-ploughs to Ethiopia. In the field of culture and of music in particular, most of the efforts undertaken by the Western countries and by international organisations, assuredly with the best of intentions, have been no less misguided, such as, for example, the creation of tenth rate symphony orchestras which replace traditional schools of the highest artistic order.

One of the results of the « colonisation » was that a group of the communities created under foreign domination gradually came to live « another life », based on a different rhythm than that of their ancestral way of life. These assimilated communities, which the former colonizers seek to support, are at the origin of the wars and conflicts which today ravage certain countries of Asia and Africa. For the modernized social classes, the amount of time which was formerly devoted to listening to and making music, has diminished to such a point that a good many musicians have pawned their instruments in order to buy an electrophone.

As in the case of all the countries whose normal development has been paralyzed and which appear, consequently, in the modern word, to be « in the process of development », the countries of Asia are attracted by the giganticism which is to be seen in the various undertakings of the Occident. People want to build cities as modern as those of America, boulevards as broad as the Champs-Elysees, and this insatiable desire for « development », born of the insolent pride which the Europeans and Americans themselves take in these spectacular accomplishments, is transferred to the field of the arts as well. One forgets that the facade of Angkor is 200 metres longer than the Palace of Versailles; what people want is to have their own symphony orchestra with the maximum number of musicians (the musical quality of the performers playing no role in these calculations.) One shrinks immediately from anything which might appear « inferior », aided in this by Western « advisers » who are often only too willing to urge the national artists along these lines – artists who would be much more in need of being directed along the path of their own culture.

Everything is done to obliterate or relegate to second place this « music of savages », as Félix Clément described it at the end of the last century in his history of music. And if this attitude is less violent today, the Western experts will do everything possible – and with the best intentions, incidentally – to replace the *vieles* with violins, and the *guimbardes* with clarinets. They will pretend that the tone of the modern instruments is far superior and the technical possibilities, as well, although this would be spurious from the point of view of the musical forms in question. At the same time, the young Oriental students allow themselves to be easily convinced that the Western scale, no matter what impression it may make upon their ears, must necessarily be superior since it has made it possible « to write » thousands of symphonies, quartets and sonatas – mysterious and magical words – and that written notation is surely the ideal means of conserving the good thematic ideas which were created in the improvisation of the preceding day.

CULTURAL PROPAGANDA

The contacts which the formerly colonised countries have kept with their former colonisers are revealed, among other things, by the broadcasting of so-called « cultural » programmes which are devised uniquely to sell the culture of the former colonisers, to the detriment of the local culture.

What the European exporter admires and proposes as

a substitute for local culture is often the most mediocre of national works. All surplus products, no longer saleable in Europe, are thrown to the countries of the Third World. The countries of the Occident do not often export the zest and ferment of their intellectual life, for that is something eternally suspect to public authorities. Art must be banal to become official. Consequently, the image which the Orient has of the Occident is often based on the simplistic and pre-fabricated ideas which English or French missionaries or the provincial petty civil servant may have of the grandeur of their national culture. Everywhere in the Orient one finds a meticulously arranged picture which depicts a pedantic, demoded, virtuous and grandiloquent Occident, scarcely corresponding with modern reality.

Having imposed their domination in various continents through the power of their armies, the countries of the Occident have, in addition, injected a certain military spirit with their arrival, and have often left a heritage of societies for parade music. Although the country was never directly colonised, this was the case in Thailand, for example, where marches and military songs were quickly adopted by the people. A publication of the Fine Arts Department (*) points out that the concerts of the « piphat » orchestra (traditional Thailand orchestra) include some « quadrilles whose tempo resembles that of a military march », and a traditional (sic) Thai melody derived from a song whose words are as follows: « Madelon's drawers have no bottom ». This song was followed, furthermore, by two others entitled, respectively, « The Hen » and « La Tremise ». Examples of this sort are numerous in all corners of the globe. After the final ceremony of Gandhi's funeral, the Indian Army Orchestra played an arrangement of « Go Up There and You'll See Montmartre » before represen-

* Thai Culture, No 16, by Fine Arts Department, Bangkok 1962.

tatives of the diplomatic corps, who were sent into fits of helpless laughter. This is a burlesque example of what has replaced the tragic accents of the *Sahnäi*. It is in any case curious to note that the first Occidental music introduced in the Orient was military music which, besides the patriotic feature of its display, was meant to give an idea of the « power » of Occidental music compared with Indian oboes, Burmese xylophones or Chinese vieles.

The kings hurried to appropriate this outward show of power in order to make of it a decorative element for parades of all sorts. The royal funerals are now accompanied by Chopin's funeral march, played by the local western orchestra at the same time that a traditional orchestra tries feebly to make its oboes heard. The military advisers encourage such procedures. To have « Madelon » played on every continent seems to be a record easy to attain, and it sums up rather well what the colonial functionaries imagine cultural propaganda to be.

II

BASIC ELEMENTS OF THE PROBLEM

PROBLEMS OF MUTUAL COMPREHENSION

A musical system to which we are unaccustomed can easily seem to be monotonous and not particularly agreeable to listen to. We may find the timbres of the voices displeasing, the tone quality of the instruments grating – and these reactions, incidentally, are quite reciprocal. We judge according to our musical habits, forms of music based on accoustical principles other than our own, and often we notice only very secondary characteristics of the music, since we are unable to perceive the essential ones. Even if we admire it, it is generally for reasons unrelated to the real value of the music, and often, we like it to the extant that it has already degenerated. A foreigner is always a bad judge of artistic matters, and when a foreigner tends to take on the superior attitudes of a conqueror, it is inevitable that he will express severe judgments on the music, exactly as he may express his displeasure with the food or the climate or the intelligence of the inhabitants. One must also take into account the ignorance and narrow-mindedness of the mediocre Westerner, who, convinced of the cultural superiority of his country, is actually as ignorant of this culture as he is stubborn in his convictions about it.

It is, however, on this basis, this presumption, that colonialism and the destruction of the civilisations of other continents have been given their moral justification. The Westerner is inclined to believe that he acts according to

Cartesian principles, and that Western thought and art are logical even if they are in error. Consequently, he considers the ways of acting and reacting on the part of other peoples, as *a priori* illogical and « backward ».

We forget too often that the monuments of Egypt were built when Europe was nothing more than a vast pre-historic field, or that the temples of Khajuraho and Angkor were flourishing well before our cathedrals were built. The situation is the same – if not more so – in the field of music. Learned theories, particularly in India, were evolved and put into practice when Europe was still at the stage of the drum-playing of *shamans*.

If we were a little more familiar with the musical theories which have brought forth the different musical languages – not only in the abstract but as profound and real human experiences – we would be able to come closer to them, instead of trying to convert them to our own ways.

For one of the principal obstacles to real understanding is the attitude of the Occidental who is always tempted to establish comparisons based upon his own concepts and who is unable, or unwilling, to put aside the various ideas acquired in the course of his education. The Occidentals believed for a long time that ways of creating music not based on solfège, chords, modes and degrees as they conceived them, were the products of an inferior art.

Evidence of this attitude is given in Félix Clément's « History of Music », published in France in 1885, in which he mentions a melody coming from Malaysia as being agreeable and « of a melancholy charm » which closely resembles « a Swedish air introduced by M. Ambroise Thomas in his opera Hamlet and sung with such success by Christine Nilsson ». The latter melody seemed to be of higher quality to him and he concludes by saying: « That is certainly a melody which the Malaysians did not invent ». And, in actual fact, he was right, because the melody was Portuguese.

It still holds true that most of the studies made on non-Western, cultivated music, as well as primitive music, are carried out by institutions which generally examine them according to identical and arbitrary criteria, no matter what musical language is being studied. It is very much as if one tried to analyze a Chinese text according to the rules of German grammar.

It is as a result of such misconceptions, absurd as they may be, that many countries of Asia are undergoing a very serious musical crisis today. Thousand year old civilisations which have developed complex and learned musical systems, musical languages which are admirably adapted to the expression of subtle and deep emotions, find themselves incapable of protecting their traditions against the influx of fruitless musical experiments from the Occident or its most banal popular art.

Many forms of Oriental music cannot be transcribed because their changeable nature does not lend itself to notation. In consequence, they cannot be preserved in books, and recordings make it possible only to preserve in fixed form some fragments, some moments as fleeting as the light on a landscape. When the last representatives of certain musical systems disappear, the loss will perhaps be as great as it would be for the West if all the music libraries were to be destroyed. For the slow but steady disintegration is synonymous with a veritable disappearance of this music, since it consists only of disparate, unlinked elements whose aesthetic cannons are in upheaval. This creates a threat to the entire musical life of a civilisation. One should imagine, in this regard, a musical world where only Occidental music reigns, encumbered by the products of its imitators from all continents, and where the dying Asian as well as the African cultures would no longer make a part of general musical life except as archeological products on records; all musical activity in Europe and elsewhere would be changed, for it is a fact that the compositions of all periods have borrowed much from the survivals of different musical languages and that young contemporary composers – they too – try to discover in the music of other cultures, new procedures and, in particular, new ideas, no matter how they use them.

They rarely realise that the music, of which they reclaim a few motifs or carve out a few fragments, represents a perfect work of art in itself. The music of the Orient is, however, as important and necessary for the West as the survivals of the musical art of the Middle Ages, which are to be found in what we call folklore, and in which so many musicians have found an inexhaustible source of inspiration.

However ,for one musical culture to contribute significantly to another, one must go deeply into its principles and not be content simply with borrowing picturesque effects of a purely external, imitative nature. It is essential that the spirit of the music be understood and that its meaning not be distorted by conceptions injected by the composers themselves. For many of them have in this way confused, in Indian music, for example, scales and modes and think that they are composing in the Indian manner and spirit because they use certain elements of the scales of the *ragas*. Furthermore, the idea of mode is much more complex.

This habit of absorbing or utilising only the external aspect of the traditional music of the Orient is noted by Jacques Chailley: « It is the haste with which a young composer – especially if he belongs to certain schools, and I am thinking especially of the otherwise so fruitful instruction of Messiaen – thinks that he has understood a music other than his own, and especially the music of the Far East, simply on the strength of a few strange elements which have the merit, to his eyes or ears, of not having cropped up in his formal studies of composition, and which he finds sufficient reason to consider that he has only to copy certain extrinsic mannerisms, without first penetrating the essence of the music ».

OCCIDENTAL ATTITUDES TOWARDS ORIENTAL CULTURES

While there has always existed a certain curiosity in the West for anything which came from Asia (for the exotic plays a very important role), this curiosity, except for very rare exceptions, has for long been tinged with incomprehension, if not with disdain. Books of former times often speak of the music of savages, and mention the Orient only for the strangeness of the instruments, without any reference to the music itself, obviously considered as primitive and without interest. This lack of comprehension is completely normal when one realises how many different aspects of a culture must be known before one can really appreciate its fruits. In the classical period, the musical conceptions of the Orient, due to thei originality, must have seemed strange indeed.

Even much later, numerous travellers have brought back diaries and memoirs filled with their impressions – always negative: the gestures of the dancers seemed like the antics of clowns, while the music was nothing more than a discordant and thundering din. Very few of the travellers found any pleasure in seeing the princely court performances of Cambodia, Indonesia or Thailand; one comes across the same comments over and over again: too much noise, instruments which sound out of tune, melodies that have no logic, etc.

In the classical period, the fashion for « Turkeries » seemed to be chiefly a comic procedure —an interlude in musical or theatrical pieces; Moliere and Mozart both made use of these *divertimenti* which so pleased the public.

In the history of Western music, one finds a few borrowings from non– European music such as Heandel's use in « The Magician of Orlando » of a pentatonic melody borrowed from the works of Pere Amiot on Chinese music. But the cases are infrequent and in all of them, there is no question of a deep understanding of the music, but quite simply the use of their tone colour, rhythm or timbre, introduced into a musical piece of quite another character. One can scarcely speak of the assimilation of Oriental music in the « Egyptian » uproars of Verdi or the « Persian » din of Ketelbey, which are simply the borrowing of external effects and which, in fact, have nothing whatever to do with the meaning of the original music from which they were taken.

This search for tonal effects, in the Romantic period, through the use of procedures supposedly borrowed from the music of the Orient, in no way changed the discomposure or lack of comprehension of even the great musicians of the time. In his « Evenings with an Orchestra », did not even Berlioz write, in his account of the Universal Exposition in London (1851), that he had heard a Chinese song: « The melody (grotesque and abominable from every point of view) finished on the tonic, exactly like one of the most vulgar of our popular romantic songs, and at no time did it depart from the key nor the mode indicated. The accompaniment consisted of a rather lively rhythmic figure – always the same – and played on the mandolin which was seldom in tune with the voice ... The Chinese and Indians would have a music similar to our own if they had any at all, but in this sphere they are plunged in the darkest shadows of barbarism and infantile ignorance, in which one can barely discern some vague and weak instincts; what is more, the Orientals call music that which we call tinkettle noises, and for them, as for the witches of « Macbeth », the horrible is the beautiful ».

Another judgment by Berlioz confirms this incapacity

for appreciation: « The Chinese sing the way dogs bark, or as cats vomit when they've swallowed a fish-bone ». Clearly, such an approach does not lead to understanding.

ETHNO-MUSICOLOGY

But the most disastrous consequences for non-Western scholarly music have been produced by a branch of learning which pretends to be new and modern: ethnomusicology. One has the impression, particularly in the case of the specialists of the preceding generation, that the musical forms which they studied and which, logically, they should cherish, were always treated with condescension. Without going back too far, we need only to open a number of the publication issued by the Musee de l'Homme (Paris), « Objets et Mondes » (Objects and Worlds) in 1967, to read in the presentation of the Museum's collection of records that « this column is devoted to the regular announcement of records of *primitive and exotic music* ». There follows a list of records among which one finds, among others, Iranian music, music of the Gamelans of Bali and the Lamas of Tibet. To regard these marvellous musical works as « exotic » shows all well the attitude and the tendentiousness with which musical art is approached here. In this connection, it is revealing and particularly striking to visit the libraries and research rooms of ethno-musicological divisions, where one can find recordings of Savoyard cow-bells, the voices of shepherds in the Pyrenees, and the *ragas* played by Ravi Shankar. And all of this under the same label because these recordings are considerd « interesting » by the « men of science », who so easily forget that between the sound of some bells (and we do not wish to deny their accoustical interest) and the music of Ravi Shankar there is a difference, and the latter, which is called music, is not a simple object of scientific curiosity, but a work of art.

It will probably always be like this, as long as university doctorate theses devoted to the epic chants of India or to the Balinese Gamelans are examined and evaluated in the framework of ethno-musicological studies instead of the history of art or of musicology, pure and simple. Only when the latter approach is adopted will Asian and African music no longer be regarded as primitive concoctions of peoples whose culture has not reached the heights of solfege. The same applies, incidentally, to all the arts where ethnography dominates. The admirable paintings on bark from Borneo have never been studied with the critical methods applied to the Italian primitives of the XVth century. The reason for this is probably because the former were studied by ethnologists and an ethnologist does not search for – or does not succeed in finding – in contrast to an artist, comprehension of the aesthetic intentions of a people, limiting his interest to the discovery of an « exotic » sociological curiosity.

Ethnomusicology has created the impression that the traditional musics were archaic survivals, about to disappear and with no longer any chance of being saved. The interest accorded this music stemmed from this fact, but diminished to the extent that it did not seem to be *worthy* of being saved. The fact that the musical cultures of Asia are generally transmitted orally from generation to generation has caused many musicologists –being good Occidentals who considered that what does not have written support cannot be perpetuated – to regard these musical forms as moribund; they fail to understand that in the first place such music, to the extent that it forms a part of the fabric of life, can, under certain conditions, be perpetuated indefinitely and can, in fact, be much more alive than written music which, on the contrary, becomes archaic to the degree that it has no close rapport with the sensibilities and language of the man of today.

A collapse of the non-written cultures has been provoked by the lack of comprehension of Occidentals of the lasting capacities of the oral traditions. It is for this reason that today it is essential to give new courage to the traditional musicians and their public who have been demoralized by a sort of cultural blackmail, which has been as persistent as it was unconscious.

And in this situation, the role of ethnomusicology, which treats this scholarly music, labelled « exotic », on the same basis as the most banal or most degenerated folk music, and tries to notate it – that is, to study it from a « civilised » point of view – has been a destructive one, to say the least. Too often, these admirers of the picturesque, who travel a great deal, record what they encounter and collect on a record the great music codified by Avicenna and Farabi, alongside the little song of a shoemaker of Kermanshah. They put together collections in which are placed side by side the brilliant technique of a classical Hindu work and the cries of Pygmy women going to market; it would be more logical, and in any case, more convenient, to have coupled certain classical Oriental works with the old music of Europe – not at all by virtue of its being old, but because in certain ways it is closer to life than contemporary music.

Musical ethnology seeks out the « primitive » and in general shows little interest in the matured and professional art as it exists, often in regions which are privileged because of their remoteness from urban or industrialised centres.

We should, however, realize to what an extent the notion of « primitive » is fallacious. Man's appearance on earth does not date from yesterday. We know that there exists no spoken language, even among populations who live today in the simplest conditions, which does not show an extremely long evolution and a complex development which makes possible the expression of the most abstract ideas. And it is difficult to see how it would be any different in the case of musical language. What one studies as being primitive, is most often only a vestige, a simplified or degenerated survival which has nothing to do with socalled archaic art. This is to be seen clearly in the structural bases even of the folkmusic idioms. These are always derived from musical systems of higly developed cultures – even if the latter have disappeared – and they are the expression of an aesthetic, as well as of the feelings, beliefs, and aspirations of a people. In no case can they be considered as a sort of phenomenon of nature which is more related to social anthropology than to musicology.

Certain efforts have been made, however, to preserve musical and dance forms which were felt to represent a « National » character. These first steps were directed toward recording. Since it was felt, however, that musical forms were being recorded which were about to disappear, nothing was done to support their perpetuation. Generally speaking, the work was carried out in the spirit of museum collectors, by ethnomusicologists foreign to the cultures under study, who did nothing to preserve what in the culture was still vital. Operating upon the principle that one is dealing with moribund music – which often happens – prevents any dynamic action which would make it possible to re-create a current of feeling in favour of the music in order to revalidate it. The attitude of pursuing an archeological job instead of a genuinely musical one has affected some of the Asians themselves, who finally begin to consider their own music as something of a curiosity for Europeans seeking exoticism. Many Orientals have arrived at the point, under Western influence, of believing that their music is really ready to be embalmed in a museum, thus accelerating the slow death of musical cultures which are still, in fact, very much alive. Ethnomusicology has created a sort of fetishism of traditions in which music is treated in the same way as are archeological remains which one must put in storage, thus putting the music, which has a role to play in life and in world art, out of the context of present reality.

THE NOTION OF FOLKLORE

One of the principal reasons that the countries of the Orient have little by little abandoned their traditional music is related to the fact that the Occident gives the impression that it considers this music as « inferior » – in believing it to be folklore which can be exploited by ethnomusicology. The benign interest shown by the dominating power in folklore is one of the masks of the sort of colonialism which we know well in Europe, for folklore is not considered to be « culture », this being a term reserved for the art of the dominating power. It is extremely difficult to prevent the person introducing a concert number from saying: « We are now going to hear Ravi Shankar interpret some Indian folk-music », or the radio announcer from saying: « The reading of poems by Hafeez is accompanied by some Iranian folk-music » when, in both cases, it is actually a question of great classical music.

It is one of the tendencies of Western musicology to give great importance to this classification into two groups – classical and folkloric – of non-European music, thus relating it to Occidental music which, with the growth of industrialized society, is separated into folk-music, which embraces all past musical cultures surviving only at the level of rural societies, and classical music, which represents the system developed for urban societies.

But in Asia, it is generally difficult to make a distinction between classical and folk music in cases where these

*

are played by the same persons and in the aggregate of a variety of social levels. In the Middle East, as in South-East Asia, it is often impossible to make this differentiation, which really belongs chiefly to the Occident. Naturally, we can, for example, speak of Court music or popular music in Laos or Thailand, but it is a purely sociological distinction and not musicological. This is because, in these cases, music is a cultural element entirely integrated into the civilisation and the basic, traditional idioms are as familiar to ordinary people as they are to members of the royal families. Furthermore, the musicians, for the most part, come from the people, and the music played in the palaces is often, though not always, a more refined version of the music which is played in the countryside. Thus, we see that the notions of « classical » and « folk » have little justification as applied to the musical art of the majority of civilisations. On the other hand, in the more industrialised Eastern societies we find the same development as in the Occident. This is true in the case of Japan, where certain aspects of the traditional Court music are no longer understood by the musicians themselves due to the fact that the rules which govern those aspects are so removed today from the spirit of modern Nipponese society, which has evolved enormously in order to adapt itself to the modern world.

The folklore of Europe, formed from the remains of old systems, often of considerable historical and artistic interest, has been studied, notated and arranged by musicians who usually had no idea of the musical forms which they were bringing into the system – we could really say, the tradition – of Guido d'Arezzo, Rameau and Helmholtz, and which they arranged in the manner of exercises of a first-year Conservatory student. It is easy enough to understand the procedure. You record a flamenco, you notate it very carefully, in the tempered piano scale, you harmonize the melody simply and then have it sung by a good soprano of international reputation in folklore, and then you compare the result with the original. The experience is conclusive and definitive. In the last 25 years, Russia has practically destroyed the admirable musical cultures of the Asiatic republics as, actually, of all the countries which it dominates, by the simple procedure of reducing the music to folklore and then reconstituting it in an arranged form.

The attitude of the 19th Century towards folk music was one of amused condescension. Folk music appeared to be a kind of musical childhood, the raw material of music which emanated from the people by a process of spontaneous generation, like a mould which forms on musty clothing. It never entered anyone's mind that one could discover, in these stammerings of musical childhood, noble and precious monuments of an ancient art whose aesthetic is exactly as justifiable as that of post-Wagnerian orchestral clamor. Composers do not hesitate to use elements of this raw material in order to make « musical works » of them, and all the while, as a rule, without appreciation of their structure or their value.

Scholars pretentiously examined these primitive expressions of the art of music with a purely scientific curiosity and used entirely inadequate methods to study this phenomenon.

If a number of the most convinced folklorists examined their consciences, they would doubtless find many remnants of those complexes which would well explain, moreover, in part, the mishaps of contemporary folklore.

As a matter of fact, we seem to have a great deal of trouble in ridding ourselves of certain notions which arise from a most stupid romantic philosophy which, unfortunately, is allied with scientific and technical progress. We jump too often without any transition, from Rousseau to Einstein. And if, in our time, one seems to attach an increasingly great importance to folklore for social, political and touristic reasons, it is done with a truly astonishing superiority complex. Thus the « restoration of folkmusic » is the infirmity of the century. Any third-class composer, belonging to the « musically educated » and hence, superior, class, feels free to arrange, to improve the most precious monuments of pre-harmonic art, with a total ignorance of what it represents and with utterly disastrous results. And few are the specialists who can recognise in the folk music which has survived, the technical, aesthetic and historical elements which enable them to understand it, correctly identify it and give it once more the place it deserves in the history of music.

We shall see that if we wish simply to evaluate the diverse forms of musical folklore from the general perspective of the history of music, we must extricate ourselves from a good number of prejudices very secretly rooted within us, of which the principal ones are the superstition of evolution, the superstition of progress, the superstition of notation and the polyphonic and orchestral superstitions.

If we wish to establish a history of music which is not limited to a few centuries of Western musical literature, we shall understand that the fundamental factor, the very basis of any history of music, rests principally on what appears today as folklore, but which is, in fact, in every period and in every country, the popular expression of the same musical language, whose learned music is simply a more highly developed and sophisticated form. The writer, the poet, the philosopher, express themselves in a language which is not, in itself, different from that of the workman or the peasant. They speak the same language at different levels. It is exactly the same in the case of folk-music, which is the popular form of a musical language which generally has its learned counterpart. The continuity of the spoken language represents the continuity, the identity of a people. And the popular language is the basis of this continuity. The superstructures are fragile and easily destroyed by wars, revolutions and foreign domination.

The continuity of a people is consequently assured by that of its popular language. The same holds true for music. The forms of folklore, over the centuries, enable us to recognise the civilisations, the migrations of peoples, the influences of cultures which have been carefully preserved in their popular forms, while the superstructures have long since disappeared. Folk music is almost always the vestige and reflection of a learned art – or is, at least, related to one. It is never created out of the blue. And it is through folklore that we can sometimes understand and find again the learned art of the civilisation of the past when sufficient elements have survived.

Very little of interest remains of Occidental folk music, to provide us with guide-lines. All countries, furthermore, take the same pains to arrange it, disfigure it, completely transform it in one way or another. There remain – just barely – a few isolated and very threatened little islands of ancient European traditional music, a few traces of Greece, in lost villages of Sicily, Calabria or Sardinia, a few reminders of Central Asia in Scotland or Brittany, a few Byzantine vestiges in our church music and few pre-Celtic vestiges in Portugal. The only living element is that admirable branch of Iranian music which they call – without quite knowing why – Canto Flamenco. But to carry out successfully a serious study of the various folklore cultures in their historical perspective, we should apply ourselves to learning their grammar and the structure of the musical language from which they came.

A melody is not in itself a musical object; it is, rather, a neutral design which can be used in any language at all and takes on, in each, a different meaning. What one calls folklore is, most often, only a simplified form of old and demoded songs which have lost their veritable musical context. The French National Radio conducted a program-

3

me on which, each morning, the producer telephoned postal employees, stenographers, provincial butchers, and asked them to sing a song. Generally, the result was a *chanson* of Gilbert Bécaud or of Sylvie Vartan, wailed in mediocre fashion, and corresponding to the original much as what folklorists reverently collect in villages corresponds to the originals of the 18th century.

Furthermore, people wish to include under folkmusic everything which differs from the Western classical idiom, even if it is of the highest professional quality and of the highest artistic value. The fundamental lack of an understanding of values leads to the absurd treatments to which the great musical traditions which still survive within the popular or folk context are subjected and which are arranged by those who understand nothing of their artistic value, to manufacture false folklore, tourist folklore, folkloric opera and other inanities which proliferate in practically every direction.

People endeavor to write down forms whose frame or system of reference they do not know, and then pretentiously teach these melodic skeletons, disfigured and mediocre, under the pretention that they are thus « saving the national folklore ».

Anyone who has had the opportunity of taking part in the traditional musical life of a non-European culture at its highest level and who has seen the folklorists and ethnomusicologists of the Occident at work, can only be astounded by the character of what interests them — the recordings, the transcriptions and the « learned » conclusions which they draw.

These disciplines — ethnomusicology and folklore — seem, with a few rare exceptions, to be oriented today towards a « research in non-culture », based on a completely demoded evolutionary concept and an idea of the inherent superiority of the musical art of the West, which, viewed from the perspective of artistic and cultural values, has no justification whatsoever. When we speak of the great systems of traditional Oriental music, it is not to refer to simple, picturesque survivals from the past. Here also there are still a great number of prejudices to combat. Too much of this highly developed music is still regarded as an object of folkloric curiosity. What should be important to us in certain Asiatic systems, is the use of principles of expression in sound which are lacking or are less developed in our own musical art; it is the use of the syntax and vocabularies of musical language which complements and differs from our own.

However, the theoretical study of these divergencies of vocabulary leads us to observe that it is not possible to isolate certain theoretical aspects of a system, from apparently external elements such as style, vocal technique, the character of the improvisation, of the composition, etcetera – all of which contribute to making a system of sounds, a means of communication and of emotional suggestiveness.

NEGATIVE ATTITUDES OF THE ORIENT

It does not suffice to place all the weight of the censure on the West for the degeneration of music in the various Asian countries. In actual fact, it seems that the latter themselves bear considerable responsibility for the situation today, although, as we have already said, their attitude can be explained by an inferiority-complex carefully nurtured.

The Fine Arts Department of Bangkok recently published a series of 12 records devoted to « national » music. But some of the recordings include « compositions » by contemporary musicians « in the traditional style », an example, no doubt, of what should be considered as the official music of this country and which, actually, present some very poor *ersatz* for a traditional music which is, quite to the contrary, very rich. One side of these records is even devoted to the recording of a local symphony orchestra of the Western genre playing some would-be modern scores, while other sides are reserved for traditional music, « revised and corrected », by orchestras assembled by the Department of Arts.

It seems that the idea of the musical profession as an exclusive metier has, in many cases, caused Asian governments to establish orchestras to integrate them into Western-type spectacles. While traditional music is generally performed under very specific and particularized conditions (outdoor performances, religious ceremonies, local celebrations, rituals, etc.) and the performers are « amateurs » from the financial and occupational point of view but professionals from the point of view of technical excellence, the establishment of orchestras whose musicians are employed full time no matter what their level of artistry, has made it possible to include the new music in the regular performances intended for foreigners. Governments think they are placing their national music in prominence by practises which are not accepted by local audiences, while uniformed Western tourists applaud these « creations », believing in good faith that they are hearing original and authentic music. It is in this way that there originates in a number of Asian countries what in called « Opera ». Using the style of traditional ballet as a basis, an old legend or a modern story is staged, with the addition of Western-type actors, usually extremely mediocre in technique and artistically disastrous. The result is catastrophic and pleases only those local people who are happy to be able to do « as they do in Europe ».

The third stage is the complete abandonment of traditional idioms in order to produce works of contemporary music of purely Western technique. At this stage only is an Oriental musician granted a significant place on the world scene. He becomes the equal of his afflictors; his symphonic works – often for reasons more political than artistic – are played by orchestras in all parts of the world. He receives prizes in international competitions. In the process of complete de-nationalization, he has acquired equal rights on the international scene.

The success of these artists – similar in every respect to the success of a European artist of equal calibre – further engenders the disappearance of traditional artists. Condemned to interest only a minority – or so they believe – they never have the opportunity of performing in halls suited to their music, or with the same advance publicity and entrance fees as those given to the other concerts. They are systematically neglected by the public powers and by concert agencies, which ignore them. And this is all the more odd since it is they who conserve the national distinctiveness which the entire country recognises as its own. But people want very much to show an interest in international music, no matter how banal it may be, while the local heritage – wich could very easily and very rapidly form a part of the international repertory – is often in a state of irreversible paralysis because of a lack of understanding that is startling. And, furthermore, it is difficult to allot the share of responsibility for this state of affairs due to the mixture of complex subjectivities which lead to this degradation of a culture, to this cultural suicide in Asian countries.

This evolution which afflicts the musical cultures today seems to result most often from an erroneous interpretation by cultural authorities, incompetent to judge what preservation of musical art truly is. In fact, Indonesia is proud of the Borobudur, as Cambodia is of Angkor and the other countries of their monuments, which, for them, stand as the very image of the genius of their peoples. Considerable sums of money are allocated for their maintenance and preservation, – not for « improving » them. But for music, it seems as if the desire to set forth this heritage takes on quite another form: it would never occur to anyone to add flying buttresses to Borobudur to imitate cathedrals. On the other hand, music, which is an art constantly in motion and impalpable, lends itself easily to all sorts of alterations. Governments therefore end up by trying to « fix » a living musical art in order to present it to audiences throughout the world, just as one makes improvements (with modern techniques) to show off Angkor. And this explains the creation of orchestras composed of musicians who learn the music « a l'occidentale » in order to present an « improved » music to the public.

Side by side with this, the setting up of chamber music groups or symphonic ensembles (almost exclusively presented during State visits or over radio chains on programmes intended for over-seas listeners, since they have little interest for local listeners), is designed to show that the countries of the Orient, in the image of European countries, are also blessed with boulevards and ultra-modern buildings ,are able as well to contribute to the music of the 20th Century, while forgetting that the living musical language of a culture is as contemporary as its spoken language.

A great effort to integrate Western music has been made by Japan. In the opinion of all the specialists, the best Japanese symphony orchestras reach the standards of the orchestras of Paris, London or New York, and in this particular aspect of music, some Japanese have chosen to adopt a foreign culture, much as some of the countries on the periphery of Europe have done. This is perfectly defensible. But for these few orchestras, with which a Menuhin or a Casadesus gladly perform concertos, how many lamentably bad groups are established elsewhere which are scarcely any better than a second-rate town band (the greater the number of musicians, the greater the noise and the more impressive it all is!). In these, one is sure to find the same number of performers as in the largest worldfamous ensembles. But what poor violinists! And what short-winded « cellists ». And all this results in a sub-culture without any real value, which cannot possibly take the place of the indigenous culture which is in danger of dying out completely.

Some composers write for their local orchestras. But what lamentable creations these are, often completely outside of the main musical currents of the time, and in which one finds everthing to please the falsely westernized Orientals: Tschaikovsky sauce stirred into Ketelbey and André Kostelanetz!

Social changes

The contributions of the West are not limited to « new ideas », to an accelerated tempo of life, or to different technical methods, which, in some cases, are more efficient. They are also to be observed in the need to simplify the different activities of living, and it is this cultural aspect of the civilisations which is the most severely affected. No one today wants to listen to − or record − a piece of music which lasts more than an hour and, here again, Asia is affected by the predominance of « digests » where people are content with excerpts and short passages. Even the most « pop » of popular songs are shortened by several verses in countries where the people feel less and less that they can « waste time ». We no longer know any young Cambodians who are willing to spend twelve years in learning to perfection the rhythms of two gongs and a drum —which the venerable old man in a distant village still knows how to perform, and with great skill. Since people have at their elbow today « music of the consumer » (radio and records), the listener becomes less demanding and less interested in making music, a phase now neglected by modern education. Instead of moving in the direction of increasingly higher development, musical art is becoming a prefab product, easily replaced, and whose quality has no importance.

The musical development taking place today in all of the countries of the Orient is particularly interesting in that it enables us to observe in a speeded-up period of a few years, a transformation which took place very gradually over a span of several centuries in the countries of the West. From many points of view, this transformation is far from revealing undeviating progress, or a constant broadening of the possibilities of musical expression. Along with the development of certain techniques, of certain methods of expression, we find the abandonment of others. We can understand, in observing today's musical adventure in the Orient, that this development is due much less to aesthetic considerations than to psychological and social factors and conditions completely unrelated to genuinely artistic values. It seems that there would be a great deal for us to gain in studying from this angle the profound revolution which caused Occidental music– as it does the music of the Orient today – to jump from a highly refined modal art to polyphony. The use of polyphony seems to have been, at the outset, a sort of game of amateurs creating an experimental music, which allowed them to treat with contempt and to replace the great musicians who represented the modal tradition.

To the extent that education develops in such a way that, from a material point of view, the populations adapt to a new mode of life which creates new demands incompatible with their traditions, music, as a product of craftsmanship, is certain to disappear unless we undertake adequate measures to save it.

Throughout the Orient, music is caught in a cross-fire: on one side, the cultural invasion of the West, which fosters hybridization or an acculturation – that is ,a change in culture; and on the other side, a brutal transformation of the pattern of life which can entail, quite simply, the disappearance of the musical language as well as of other arts and techniques. Japan is an extreme example of the development of a belief in a nation that it could vanquish the West only in its own terms. Japan's musical life is highly developed, every big city has its symphony orchestra and numerous chains of radio and TV broadcast classical and light music all day long. The Japanese have apparently adapted themselves so well to the ways of the West that their traditions seem no longer to be anything but a veneer, and the genuine music of Japan can hardly find performers to interpret it. There are fewer and fewer musicians to play it and a smaller public to listen to it, but it is important to note that certain artists and intellectuals have recently become concerned about the possible extinction of their traditional music and that a great effort is being made today to revive and increase the activities in the field of ancient music.

It has however become set and rigid and is treated like a museum piece. It has lost all its own power of renewal. Japan has demonstrated that the techniques and arts of the Occident are available to all the peoples – free for the taking – but in taking them, Japan has lost some of its own soul.

It could happen that the progressive abandonment of a traditional music was caused by a definite psychological break which makes it impossible for the native people to readjust to the art forms on which their culture is based. In numerous countries aluminium or plastic receptacles have replaced the admirable pottery made by hand and varnished by very refined and subtle methods. People destroy these types of pottery because they now seem unattractive and useless – until the day that they find their place in the museums.

The same is true for the music. People prefer the glowing tones of the violin, the sound of which carries far, to the frail twostringed viol of South East Asia with its weaker resonance (we must underline the fact that almost always, preference is given to a music or an instrument because of its sound volume). Even the lute sound-boxes are replaced by transformed metal ones. We have already spoken of the misdemeanors of the loud-speaker, which, in the eyes of Asiatics, has the merit of benefiting everybody – from a single sound source. It is sufficient to see the obvious satisfaction of everyone when, in Indonesia or elsewhere, noisy musical din is broadcast during celebrations over the loud-speakers from the small ritual enclosure or from the village square. It is no longer surprising, either, to hear Ray Charles or Edith Piaf at the same moment, crying forth from two neighboring houses while a *dalang* remains true to his tradition in manipulating the marionettes of his shadow-theatre a few feet away.

The industrial superiority developed by the Occident is undeniable and will constantly work against the currents of those civilizations which are of a less well-equipped standard of technical efficiency, if not of culture. At the same time, the temptation of the peoples of the Orient to take over everything that seems modern – a word which has become almost synonymous with Occidental – is too great to give us hope that much help can be given, unless it might be through a consideration of cultural values on an international scale, independent of economical or technical values. Nicolas Nabokov has these comments to make on the repeated failure of the numerous attempts already made in this direction: « To pretend and give oneself over entirely to the illusion that one can patch the dike to prevent the ancient traditions from being inundated by tendencies which are equally ancient and which develop with great rapidity in Western music, would be a Utopia that we should cease trying to maintain. The modern world with its popular and sophisticated music will penetrate, if only because of its financial resources, these ancient reserves of artistic beauty, serenity and feeling. The modern world is a brutal monster, with a great deal of strength and freshness and is entirely without pity or compassion. Furthermore, it is a world in a hurry, with rapid decisions, with thoughts fabricated by computers, and with the mass media which moulds the spirit – and, as Mcluhan has said it so well, " massages " it ».

The public's indifference

Does what is called « new music » interest Oriental listeners? Probably not more than one in a million. But it interests the governments and the propaganda services and, because of this, the composers and performers, who work in the Western idiom or make so-called experiments, receive privileges and honours out of all proportion to those received by the greatest musicians who persevere in the national musical idiom, although the latter are the only ones, in fact, who could be presented in the great international halls. Great efforts will be made to impose the new music on the public, who, for lack of anything else, will end up, unwillingly enough, by getting used to it.

This state of mind arises from the necessity of the countries of the Orient to « modernize » themselves and to show themselves the equal and the rival of the Occident, even in the field of artistic productions. It was a result of a misunderstanding, whose origin is entirely due to the ignorance of the Western colonialists, to their refusal to study and respect other cultures, that the countries were reduced to denying their own culture, though, in fact, many artistic performances of the Orient (in music and in dance) belong to our universal artistic heritage on the same plane as many forms of Occidental art. Let us not forget the phrase that we hear every day: « Oh, he's a charming, cultivated and intelligent African who speaks French perfectly, is interested in literature (French), in politics (French) and in music (European), etc. ».

The result of this Occidental prejudice tends to bring about a complete destruction of the native cultures. This is all the easier since the international musical ideal becomes more abstract, gives as little place as possible to sensitivity, to emotion – to the aesthetic in which the characteristics of racial or cultural personality might risk re-appearing.

The modern musical compositions produced in the countries of the Orient, and which are for the most part impossible to listen to in Europe, are as quickly forgotten as they are written, for they represent nothing of the experienced or felt patrimony. These compositions, like the orchestras which perform them, offer only a pale imitation of Europe, and they are presented by these de-nationalized Asiatics, who today make up almost everywhere the ruling class and who try to persuade themselves that the Occident is in all aspects the symbol of beauty and progress and modernism, even in the world of music, for if it were not the case, their way of life and their politics would become or be regarded as criminal. But, actually, the Occident which they imitate has long since become passé and for more than a century the civilications of the Orient have been struggling with a strange phantom of an imaginary Occident – which is ridiculous and completely démodé. We must recognize, however, that this phantom is very active and that it has repeated so often to the Iranians, the Hindus, the Turks and the Cambodians that their music is monotonous, that they have not yet discovered harmony, which is presented as the panacea for all ills, that these peoples no longer dare, except in secret, to listen to the works of their own classic art for fear of being considered mentally underdeveloped. The most courageous simply break off completely with tradition; virtuously, they renounce all the pleasures and joys of their music and devote themselves to the creation of absurd orchestras because someone told them that the music of all civilized people requires them to be, above all, very big. It is this attitude which brings it about that many Asian countries insist on having their own symphony orchestras or their own ballet group of the Western classical sort, whose stars would make the youngest beginners in Paris or Vienna burst with laughter. In spite of all the good intentions of these efforts, they are inevitably destined to disaster. And it is unfortunately the result of these efforts which they try to present to the foreigner — with a kind of childish pride; while the foreigner comes to visit a country where he expects above all to come upon performances of a culture completely different from his own.

It is this profound uneasiness which explains why the Asiatic governments are so opposed to allowing their truly great artists to represent them abroad. They fear that they will be misunderstood, and the insult made to their own real culture will wound them too deeply. They prefer to see this culture die rather than to see it mistreated, for the secret hurt would then be too deep.

Instead of giving the great Iranian musicians even a modest means of living and honouring them, the government has preferred to build an opera house, although there are no orchestra or singers of a passable standard, and although everywhere else the provincial opera houses have been turned into movie houses. Such silly actions reveal a dangerous psychological crisis.

In many cases, as far as local music is concerned, all psychological response has disappeared to such a degree that a musical re-education becomes a necessity in order to teach people how to listen. Some Japanese, particularly receptive to the West, have forgotten their own music to such an extent that the competent authorities felt the need to set up a policy specifically for bringing about a return to their musical sources. In this case it is really a question of life-saving, as Professor Shigeo Kishibe has expressed it: « The activities of the Academy of Arts and of the National Commission for the Protection of Cultural Patrimonies do not only succeed in encouraging professional musicians but serve also in awakening the interest, in general, of the public. In spite of all the efforts made in disseminating the material, the decadence of traditional music in Japan has been scarcely halted at all. We Japanese need the advice of those abroad who will tell us how important the tradition of each nation is – how necessary it is to the creation of music, both of that nation and of the whole world ... We well remember the case of the Ukiyoe, those woodcuts, whose value was recognized in Japan only after foreigners had appreciated them ».

THE USE OF MODERN TECHNIQUES

All over the world – and particularly in Asia – the strong impression which the passing tourist can carry away with him is the countless number of transistor sets to be seen in operation in every region of the country. One can no longer go into the jungle or on a fishing raft in the middle of a lake, or in the rice fields far away from all settlements, without hearing a heavy dose of « pop » music. As on our own over-crowded beaches, everyone parades about with his transistor in hand and becomes accustomed to living in an increasingly loud and noisy sound environment, which destroys the ear's sensitivity and the faculty of concentration. The transistor has become the distraction of everyone – at a very cheap price – and even among very poor people, there are few families who do not have a set of their own. In any case, it is the first important expenditure to be made in each home. Far be it from us to give the impression that we do not believe in the usefulness of technical developments. The transistor is extremely important – especially in isolated and distant regions – as a means of contact. It is, rather, on the use made of it, the kind of programmes which the radios broadcast over it, that there is a great deal to be said. For the moment, let us simply say that its parasitic role is now well-established in the customs of all the peoples of the world. The governments which spend enormous sums for education, for the schools, the universities, the museums, do not seem to have realized that the education of children, adolescents and adults, is effected today chiefly by radio, television and records. It is from these sources that information, tastes and knowledge come. It is from them that people form their idea of the world and of life. The purpose of the theatre in Asia was, earlier, to form people's characters by the example of heroes and gods. The technical media seem today to have as their purpose to abolish culture instead of to serve as its means of communication. To maintain in a society the taste for its own culture necessitates keeping the people in touch with it. It is in doing this that the modern technical media could be most useful: the radio can and should be of great assistance when one considers the enormous means of propagation at its disposal. It must be acknowledged that a few countries have made an effort and now give an important place (and time) to the broadcasting of local music over the national networks.

In Cambodia, for example, half of the listening time reserved for music is devoted to khmer music while a TV programme devoted to traditional arts, principally dancing, is organized by the University of Fine Arts. These broadcasts are realized within the framework of a broad programme devoted to the arts in general. But it is to be feared that due to the increasingly loud demands of a minority of citizens who wish to play at being Europeans and listen to more Occidental light music, the national radio may be forced to cut down the time given to traditional music to make place for so-called modern music – that is, for chansons and « pop ». The problem is essentially the same in all the Asian countries where modern music – principally light music, that is – is particularly sought for in the cities, while the rural areas remain faithful to the traditional conception of music, serious and subtle.

Another essential aid to the situation would be putting on the market, at a price accessible to everyone, numerous books and records dealing competently with the various musical cultures: obviously they must be of the highest quality. In some collections of Asian music records for example, the editors mix together art music with folk music, as if we might bring out on the same record a Brahms sonata and a song of the Vendée market-gardeners. From this point of view, it is indispensable that the choice of recordings be made with competence and discrimination. Similarly, the explanatory text must be sufficiently precise and explicit to give the reader a comprehensive view of the musical art of a particular musical culture and without being forbiddingly scholarly, it should provide guidance to those who are interested in going further into the question by suggestions of a more technical bibliography.

Records have an important role to play in directing public taste – in the Occident as well as the Orient – and it is indispensable to make use of this marvellous means of communication to lead the Occident to revising its attitude towards non-European music. Thanks to a fairer dissemination, the musical cultures of the Orient, as well as those of other continents, should, in the long run, find again their place in the field of universal culture.

There exists in the Western world a superstition about writing. Written proof plays an important role in our reasoning and in forming our convictions. We seek a written precedent for any assertion and we attribute a sort of magic value to a written document.

The superiority accorded to everything which is written or noted down is enhaced by the results which writing has made possible in other fields – in the sciences, in particular and in their applications. The place given to musical notation, however, in relation to the phenomenon of sound, and to the composer in relation to the performer, seems to be extremely exaggerated in the Occident. Notation does not enable us to record a living music with sufficient precision to retain its real meaning from the point of view of the history of musical languages. It records only the structures which the performer must complete and bring fully to life. The relative role of the structural element which can be notated and the creative element which depends upon the performer-interpreter varies considerably according to the musical languages. Writing leads to the development of structural elements in music to the detriment of expressive and imaginative elements. One should remember in this connection that theoretically very small differences of intonation can differentiate fundamentally between musical styles and « families ». Real analysis of musical styles can only be made on the basis of musical semantics in which sound is not isolated from its content, its meaning, its place in the theory of communication. Expressive sound presents considerable and almost indefinite possibilities of differentiation, which sound, empty of meaning, does not possess. The case for music is quite completely analogous to that for the spoken word. The difference between the diction of a good actor and a bad one is slight in terms of the sounds emitted. The difference in meaning is immense. The notation and analysis of the differences in the sounds emitted are, however, almost impossible. Consequently, in the analysis of music, we must always be wary of measures taken without an expressive context, for they are inevitably inexact. Any attempt at analysis which might contribute some precise elements about the nature of a musical system and the family to which it belongs must be made on a live and expressive performance, with semantic content, and for this the possibilities of modern recording techniques provide the means to renew completely our analytical methods and, incidentally, our whole conception of the study of musical languages, for transcriptions have inclined musicologists to reduce material to a neutral and amorphous common denominator represented by the musical staff; the latter fits everything into the inadequate limitations of a 12-tone scale. The efforts to analyse musical systems through notated music have been up to now much too imprecise and arbitrary to make possible a better understanding of the different modes of sound communication. For it is, in fact, by studying in greatest detail the form, structure and extension of an ornament or of an attack in a live performance that we can determine the nature and characteristics of a particular musical language and not by notating approximately the main lines of a melodic development, deprived of these characteristic elements of style, intonation and meaning.

We must beware of the superstition of notation and of the dangers it holds. Only a very small fraction of the world's music can be transferred to paper. Notation is applicable chiefly to Occidental music of a certain period – which, because of this device, this possibility, has developed in a form which is very much its own. As Jacques Charpentier has remarked, « When, at the end of the Middle Ages, the Occident attempted to notate musical discourse, it was actually, only a sort of shorthand to guide an accomplished performer, who was, otherwise, a musician of oral and traditional training. These graphic signs were sufficiently imprecise to be read only by an expert performer and sufficiently precise to help him find his place if, by mishap, he had a slip of memory. Consequently, as we see, it was not a question of a precise notation but rather a mnemonic device in written symbols. Later on, the appearance of the musical staff, on the one hand, and symbols of time duration on the other, made it possible to move on to a real notation which reflects with exactitude the whole of the musical material presented in this manner. At this point in history, it does not seem as if the contemporaries of that time fully realized the consequences of their discovery. For, in actual fact, from that moment on, a musical work was no longer strictly musical; it existed outside itself, so to speak, in the form of an object to which a name was given: the score. The score very soon ceased to be the mere perpetuator of a tradition to become the instrument of elaboration of the musical work itself. Consequently, the analytical qualities of musical discourse took precedence in the course of centuries over its qualities of synthesis and the musical work ceased to be, little by little, the expression of an experienced psycho-physiological continuum – on the spot and at the moment it is experienced; and instead, became what is more and more prevalent today in the Occident – that is, a willful, formal and explicative construction which finds in itself alone its substance and its justification ».

Even for Occidental music, notation is far from being a precise expression of a work. It gives no indication of certain nuances which the interpreter contributes; and these nuances give a communicable meaning to what was merely a well-constructed score. In fact, between what is written and what is played, there is a great difference, and many details simply cannot be indicated since it is a question of interpretation and this varies with each interpreter. A mechanical performance of a score leaves out certain essential aspects of the music. But the superstition about notation is so anchored in Western ways that musicologists cannot detach themselves from it in the studies they undertake on the various musics of the Orient, which, for the most part, through their very nature, develop precisely in that zone of musical art where the possibilities of notation do not exist. Miles and miles of music manuscript have been filled with notated African or Asian musics, but it is difficult to see up to now of what value all the work has been.

It is interesting to note furthermore, that in the case of some contemporary music such as concrete music and electronic music, notation tends to disappear again to enable the composer to create less rigid structures. These, if their postulates were less abstract and more in conformity with the audio-mental norms, should make possible a rediscovery of certain aspects of the phenomenon of music. In the countries where music is written, we preserve documents and a contact with part of the musical history and heritage, although we often remain very ignorant about the style and interpretation of the older works. Modern experiments are only of relative value. But in the Asian musical forms, of which very few elements can be practically transcribed, the transfer of interest to a new international idiom could well cause, with the loss of oral transmission of traditional music, the complete obliteration of the local cultures – and in consequence, the loss of an important part of the cultural heritage of humanity. This is not an event which we can envisage with a light heart.

HYBRIDIZATION

Well-maintained by the powerful forces of radio broadcasting, hybridization, which can be observed essentially in a tendency to superimpose certain characteristics of one system on another, began to develop with the introduction of industrial civilization. All of the musical forms are touched by it, whether the art music, folk music or light music. A tendency to standardization is expanding identically in the countries of the Orient and the Occident, gradually eliminating the individual character of the different musical languages, which lose their style and expressive power without gaining anything of value in their place. People harmonize melodic forms derived from a modal system so that they may be played by modern orchestras or by artificial formations which are sometimes called « typical orchestras », without apparently realizing that harmony and mode are incompatible. There exist indissoluble relationships between style, instrumental workmanship, melodic or polyphonic characteristics of a given music, which form a whole – adapted to the expressive intentions belonging to each system. It is only the most external aspects which come into play when a given music is adapted to a standardized idiom. The process of hybridization has been analyzed by Zaven Hacobian, Director of the Iranian Ministry of Culture:

There is first of all the influence of conceptions of form. It seems to me that this has been a little neglected and its importance underestimated in the studies and discussions devoted to the subject up to this time. We know that in the forms belonging to the traditions of Oriental art music, the melodic development is not carried out by developing a precise theme in the manner of Occidental music. It is achieved, rather by a subtle discourse which consists of giving importance successively to each of the steps of the given scale. These steps become, one after the other, by clever maneuvers, the centre and axis of all the melodic « action », creating and expressing, in succession, very clearly defined emotional states and impressions, with their particular colours and their expressive meaning. It is in this way that, within the limits – within the enclosure – of a single, main system (called in Persian « dast-gâh »), a multitude of secondary modal combinations (called in Persian « gouchés ») are created.

This work in finest detail, which, strictly speaking, can be considered as the development of the notes of the scale, has, actually, little in common with the procedures followed in the development of a theme and does not include the return of thematic material in the Western manner. This form of development, consequently, has scarcely any Occidental equivalent.

The influence of Occidental formal concepts can be observed in our traditional forms in different ways: there in imitation or adaptation of the principles of thematic structures and the use, more or less conscious, of forms of foreign origin. But there is also – and in particular – that tendency to shorten, to « concentrate » the traditional development of a system and to neglect certain secondary modal combinations, a tendency not to respect the order of succession of these combinations, which was established by the laws of tradition. And the reason for this has been chiefly to accentuate very distinct melodic entities, often allowing the return of thematic material which is easy to recognize and to follow. In this tendency a movement away from the traditional spirit, as far as structures are concerned, is undeniable; Occidental influence is no less so, although a little hidden.

Hybridization in forms is likely to have much more complex consequences than those we can first observe. It is awkward to try to evaluate the extent and importance of the problem of formal hybridization by isolating it and by making an abstraction of the other elements of the whole of a musical tradition. For is is clear that formal hybridization can be at the same time either the cause or the effect.

The inclination to harmonize or polyphonize is probably the best known form of hybridization. In dealing with this problem it is important to recall some of the charcteristics of the art music of the Orient. We know that it is, in its classical and traditional forms, essentially monodic and homophonic. It has developed over the centuries and almost always exclusively and essentially in a melodic sense; the temptation to use polyphony has been chiefly theoretical.

As a French musicologist once put it – and not without reason – in the West we construct solid blocks of music. After having carved out geometrically, in large sections, like building stones, the seven degrees of the diatonic scale; one lined them up and placed them on top of each other according to cleverly worked out architectural laws which are called counterpoint and harmony. And in this way one erected splendid edifices in sound. In the East, no one dreamed of dividing sound into blocks; instead, they refined it to a wirethin thread. They strove meticulously to stretch out the sound, to refine it to the point of extreme delicacy ... No standardized materials, no buildings of two or six or ten floors; rather, a simple, variegated silk thread which unwinds and rises and falls imperceptibly but which in every tiniest portion evokes a world of feelings and sensations.

Thus, we see that some musical systems have been formed and developed which have inner relationships, intervals and scales, derived from quite other principles than those which are current today in the Occident. It was the first direct contacts with Western musical concepts that brought with them the first attempts at harmonization and, in a general sense, at polyphonic adaptation. The most naive sort of hybridization, so to speak, consists in bending the modes of traditional music to the demands and rules of classic, tonal harmony ... In doing this, for example, certain modes were thus adapted – modes whose dominant, in the Occidental sense – is not necessarily the fifth degree, modes in which the note having the character of a leading-tone is not the seventh degree, or whose first degree does not fulfill the functions of the tonic; to say nothing of their scales or their particular cadences ... The results of this operation, it is clear, could show only the most distant relationship with these traditional modes – to such a degree that even the use of the term hybrid in describing them sometimes seems scarcely applicable or justifiable.

Another tendency in hybridization – more justifiable than in the one just described – consists of finding and using new chords and harmonic combinations – not in accordance with the rules of classic, tonal harmony but in taking into account the particular modal characteristics, thus utilizing to advantage the « personality » of the principal, generating notes, the cadences and the characteristic flow of the melody and its development according to each case. Some people have also tried harmonic combinations making use of so-called quater-tones or in imitating this particular effect, even going so far in this field as building up specific theories. (Congress of Shiraz, 1968).

Zaven Hacobian continues:

More recent and more suitable is the contrapuntal and polyphonic tendency which attempts to derive from the traditional modes themselves melodic lines to accompany them appropriately and to « enrich them » horizontally. The danger of a « clash », so to speak, between the typical modal characteristics and the procedures of polyphonic combinations are less in this case and, on the other hand, since the approach and the general conception are horizontal and melodic, the problems which arise can often be resolved by means which are neither essentially foreign to the traditions nor totally incompatible with them; one comes across a number of realizations which are, artistically speaking, more or less successful, thanks to this procedure.

All these procedures overlook the essential aspect – namely that a traditional work is a perfect work of art in itself and that attempts to adapt or use certain elements from it leaves nothing of the quality and value of the original. The influence of Occidental conceptions is seen also in the field of instrumental and vocal techniques, particularly in regard to style and interpretation. This is true, for example, in the case of certain modern Chinese operas, in which the singers interpret (already hybridized) melodies with voices of tenors or sopranos, whereas their vocal technique was adapted to the possibilities of their spoken language (levels of tone) as well as to the demands of their musical language. In these new adaptations there remains little that is genuinely Chinese except in the title and the language, and it is hard to say whether the music is Asiatic or Occidental. In the 1950's symphonies and concertos « on Sinkiang themes » or from other provinces flourished – analogous to certain attempts made by some Western composers to use Oriental themes and procedures. In actual fact, the words « harmony » and « polyphony » have become slogans which are regarded as synonymous with highly-developed, civilized music. People search everywhere for traces of polyphony, for the beginnings of polypony, as if it were incontestable that the polyphonic stage in the development of music is superior and a higher level of development. This is why people wish at any cost to harmonize modal music even though it is absolutely contrary to its nature. They try to harmonize, to reform, to develop, to Borodinize, to Stokowski-ize a music which up to then had seemed so gentle, so perfect, so that it might, nominally at any rate, be compared with the music which symbolizes the power of the Occident. And from this attitude has come the idea of training national composers who will « renovate » the local music. Convinced as they are that progress arrives by evolution (but evolution is understood here as being an imitation of the Western manner) the Asian governments persuade themselves that it is necessary to « renovate » their music and no longer to allow it to be transmitted orally, for the nobility decrees that anything of real value should be written and musical art must necessarily « develop » the use of a score. And, in this way, they come to treat the great musicians like great fashion designers from whom people expect a new style each season. To accomplish this, the musicians attach one melodic phrase to another, and top off the whole with a few taps on the drum and some moaning noises on the clarinets. One gets a « made in China » concerto which the local artists will try to make famous but it will never be able to win over an Occident which inevitably remains indifferent to a music without interest.

The renovators of music need great courage in carrying out their task, for the din which results from their efforts is no less painful to their ears than it is to our own. Brochures are even published in certain cases to explain how much a traditional orchestra has been improved by the addition of the vibraphones and xylophones of jazz, and this, they say, is the only way to make their music « develop ». For, one of the deep regrets of the persons responsible for the artistic life of these countries is to have in their country a music which does not develop, seems always alive and new and, nevertheless, does not change its basic principles. It amounts to a complex which causes people to regard everything that seems stabilized as retrogressive and not worthy of the 20th Century. People speak today of « finding a new style », of « improving » the instruments and of « composing » traditional music – and the latter is, of course, a contradiction in terms. It looks as if the directors of artistic policies have not yet understood that improvisation inevitably includes a development, an expression of modern sensibilities.

The hybridization of the musics of Asia can be active in many different ways. The main influence seems to come from light music and its easily remembered rhythms. It is this very facility – which is not regarded as a high quality anywhere – which particularly favours the penetration of light Western music in the Asian countries of highly developed traditional culture. Beginning with the easily remembered rhythms among the young of all countries, there results a sort of « mélange » of the media of expression: one can sing a modern popular song accompanied by a traditional orchestra. In the new « Mohori » music of Cambodia, to the contrary, a traditional song is « enriched » by a « modern » accompaniment. The same is true for all the music for the dance which one can hear in South-East Asia – it is simultaneously a mixture of jazz, fashionable rhythms and the pentatonic scale. This development comes about effortlessly and placidly since the radio incessantly broadcasts popular songs and these become the musical norm. This occurs all the more easily in that many young people often play both a traditional instrument and a European instrument – the latter enabling them to earn their living by playing in dance halls or at festive celebrations.

As for the art music, it is sometimes deformed by its own protagonists. This occured in a case cited in 1967 by Mehdi Barkeshli:

For half a century now the scholarly circles have been adapting to the reform of Iranian music decreed by Nassereddin Shah Kadjar, who requested one Mr. Lemaire to organize Iranian military music. This French musician had the idea of transcribing several modes of Iranian music into the Occidental idiom. This idea was strongly supported by Ali-Naghi Vaziri, the great master of the Tar, who, very much influenced by Occidental music, tried to harmonize his compositions. He ran into difficulties, particularly in transposition, because the Iranian scale contains unequal intervals! and he wished in spite of everything to retain, to a certain extent, the essential characteristics of the Iranian modes. Therefore, he proposed a division of the octave into twenty-four quarter tones, all equal, in imitation of the Western tempered scale of twelve semitones. This system has evolved and has been imposed as a system of instruction at the Conservatory for the last fifty years. The traditional methods are absolutely excluded from official instruction. Consequently, the orchestras and nonpopular musical forms are hybrid. Most of the radio and TV musical programmes as well as the music for official occasions is composed in this way.

The Javanese and the Cambodians have experienced the visits of musicians from Europe who have wanted to help them tune their instruments – musicians who were touched to observe that these innocent peoples had not discovered the consonance of the open fifths, while, in reality, they tuned their gamelangs on very different principles – and more scientific ones – principles of which the well-meaning Occident had never even heard. As a result of this sort of misunderstanding, in most non-European countries, one witnesses a series of concerted efforts, most often unconscious and well-meant, on the part of governments, radios and music schools as well as « experts » of international organizations to deform and subsequently destroy great traditional music under the pretext of preserving the national art by helping its evolution and by modernizing its basic ideas. Methods of instruction are changed. They force the musicians, who are usually soloists, to play in ensembles, in improvised orchestras, contrary to all their customs, all their musical conceptions – and all of this in the hope that the result will be the least disagreeable as possible and will resemble a little – but not too much, for it must still be national – tangos and rock 'n roll, for that is the ritual music which pleases the gods of today. People are also seized by the madness of gigantism. They want the traditional orchestras to reach dimensions which will thus overcome the inferiority complexes of these musicians in confrontation with Western philharmonic orchestras. Out of a traditional orchestra, in which each instrumentalist improvises on a given theme, they form an orchestra in which each instrument is multiplied by ten in order to obtain a total which approaches the number of musicians in the Berlin Philharmonic, hoping in this way to dazzle the foreign tourist who will only then be able to make a favorable comparison of the greatness of the civilizations. They also alter the use of voices, and instrumental techniques, not using as models any of our great performers – that would be too difficult – but the most simplistic styles of Italian, French or American popular songs, of which the records are most often the only ones that the noisiest representatives of the Occident bring with their gramophones in the course of their civilizing missions.

In some areas the radio has contributed most notably to deforming the traditional music. One case in point, among others, is Thailand where a hybrid music has been created (local music played on Western instruments or Western music on local instruments), created no doubt with the praiseworthy intention originally to please the foreigners living in this country. Any alteration of this sort, furthermore, pleases most listeners immediately: the Occidentals, first of all, because of the facile exoticism of this music, and the local people thereafter, who accept immediately any novelty which seems more « modern ». Furthermore, there are numerous radio stations which foster hybridization. This has happened in Iran, for example, where they have set up small orchestras of traditional instruments and where simplified Iranian melodies are sung by sopranos. But all of these musics reach a public imbued with its local culture and intellectually defenceless against what comes from outside. The new music is first accepted rather unwillingly, as people accept foreign domination, and then it penetrates little by little into customs of everyday life and especially among the young.

In Libya, they tried to codify and collect diverse elements of local folklore and immediately adapted it for orchestras of Occidental type. These diverse traditions of ancient music and Arab music are mixed together in a vague, exotic, musical salad, in which nothing of the values of the original systems survives.

The Western type of orchestras and the orchestral adaptations of Indian music in Indian radio programmes are becoming increasingly important, but there has also been the beginning of reaction. Half of the musical programmes are today devoted to the « classic » musical art of the different states.

INSTRUMENTS AND PERFORMANCES

The uniformization of techniques goes hand in hand with an artistic uniformization, even though the latter is of a different order. One can observe this in the case of the slow but irremediable evolution of musical instruments. As an example, we may quote from an article – already quite old – devoted to different instruments of Khmer music, published by a tourist office and reproducing a text written in 1930 by a French military man:

referring to the Takké (3-stringed cithar), two strings are used for the melody, beautiful and low. The other could be used as bourdon but is not of much use today. Nowadays, the player uses only three fingers. It is not sufficient. This instrument could have its possibilitiens increased by tho fifths if the players of Takké, through a modicum of effort to get out of their rut, would use all their fingers. If the player used the thumb of his right hand to play on the low string, the bass sound would be of the same timbre as that of the high note (. . .) and finally, a simultaneous attack of the bourdon string and the other two could eventually sketch some harmonies. (Referring to the Trô-khmer, a plucked vièle with three strings) the hair of the Cambodian bow is held by the fingers of the player between the hair and the wood of the bow. This instrument is so difficult to play . . . that it would be good to put a stretcher on the khmer bow so that we will not see this most beautiful traditional instrument of Cambodia disappear.
(In speaking of the *Sralay*, oboe) If Cambodian music develops as far as the symphony, it will be necessary to enable it to modulate and add the tonalities.
(Regarding the *roneat*, the xylophones) . . . the players

could usefully employ two sets of hammers, for the hard hammers only produce « empty » sounds. What is needed is a set of hammers which make it possible to hear the fundamental tone. By using these two sets of hammers alternately the instrument would be enriched by impressive effects.

After reading these examples, one can more readily believe that an officer of the French navy, with all the authority which his « knowledge of solfège » conferred upon him, might have been able, around 1940, to have all the musical instruments of the Royal Palace of Phnom-Penh retuned according to the tempered scale – the superiority of which permitted no questioning.

Often, the local musicians, influenced by Western ideas, use their ingenuity to make new instruments or to transform the tradition instruments in such a way that the new sounds they acquire no longer have anything in common with those of the original instrument. It seems as if in this field too we find a mania for gigantism. For example, the 17-stringed koto invented by Michie Myagi, is much larger than the ordinary koto. The sarangi double-basses made today in India and especially tars or the giant kémantchés of the « folkloric » orchestras in the U.S.S.R. are puerile imitations of the instruments of the European orchestra. Since the main concern is generally to swell the volum of sound, a good many transformations towards this end concentrate on the development of resonators when, more simply, they don't use a microphone. The originally silk strings are little by little being replaced by metal strings like those of European guitars; this has happened in the case of the Chinese *tseng* and the Korean *kayakoum*. And nowadays one even uses nylon strings for the Cambodian *tro* and *cha-pey*. The reeds of Laotian *kens* are now made of silver and no longer of bamboo. In addition, it is not rare to come across the intrusion of Occidental instruments in the traditional orchestras. The violin in India or Viet-Nam, the banjo in Cambodia, are gladly included in traditional group although they add nothing from a musical point of view. It would probably be better not even to mention the deplorable harmonium. Certainly the most striking example occurred in the « Fine Arts Department » of Thailand, where the instruments of the Piphat orchestra were replaced by their Occidental homologues; vibraphones, clarinets, cymbals, triangles, etc., and the result, as one could well expect, was disastrous. The melodic forms become rickety and stiff and have only a distant connection with their originals.

It is appropriate to emphasize here the importance of the intimate relationship which exists between workmanship and technique, on the one hand, and everything which characterizes a musical tradition. The technique and the workmanship of the instruments are always adapted and made appropriate to the expressive intentions of all the elements of a system or of a tradition, and their evolution and their perfectioning have moved in this direction.

In many Oriental countries, certain traditional instruments have been abandoned – have often even disappeared – and have been replaced by Occidental instruments which, externally, resemble the originals. This in true in the case of the kémantché, for example, a Persian bowed instrument which has been replaced by the violin. It is true that, in this case, a particular technique and style were created and which seem adapted to the expressive necessities of Persian music. One speaks of the violin « à la iranienne ». Nevertheless, the alteration of the timbre and other particularities belonging to the original instrument, confront us with a type of hybridization, a gradual transformation of the style. We must emphasize at this point the important initiative of the Iranian State Secretariat of the Fine Arts, which for several years, has been trying to revive the kémantché, that was beginning to disappear, and to encourage and spread its use more widely.

It is in undertaking an action of this sort, which, at first glance one might regard as retrogressive, that true « progress » in musical art is to be found.

The vibraphone with electric blower is coming to replace the metallophones and xylophones in certain countries of the Far East. The guitar, particularly, is becoming more widely used and replaces the traditional lutes; and when these guitars are electric the balance is thrown off in the relationship with the other instruments of the orchestra.

The use of wind instruments presents a similar case. The flute and clarinet are replacing instruments of the same type but the latter possess more extensive and varied technical and practical possibilities, always adapted to the necessities of a subtle and ornamented melodic style. It is sufficient to listen to the prodigious technique of a Bismillah Khan on an instrument apparently as « primitive » as the sahnaî, to realize that no European oboe could produce such tonal effects. One should also mention the use of an instrument which could not be more completely Occidental – the piano, tuned in such a way that, for better or worse, non-tempered scales could be played on it. There is also the trumpet, with mute, and the use of electic amplification for certain instruments of weak volume. The transformations in singing technique and vocal style change the potentialities of the voices, and they can no longer perform the melismas characteristic of the different musical genres.

In Thailand one now sees quite frequently lutes whose sounding box has been made of various containers. Old double bass cases bought at a second-hand market are transformed into sounding boards for stringed instruments. Finally, the reeds are replaced by metallic tubes which are more resistant. These « transformations » are not yet systematic, but they will be dangerous if they become more widespread in the future. They show, in any case, that the musicians, after coming in touch with Occidental instruments, lose their perceptivity for nuances of instrumental timbres and succeed only in carrying through the realization of the melodic phrase – the only thing that they distinguish with certainty when they listen to Occidental music.

Instrumental hybridization and the abandon of improvisation are two of the principal dangers which threaten the musics of Asia; and yet, people have tried with as much incompetence as good faith to improve the manufacture of the instruments. In a South East Asian country, once, students, on leaving their solfège classes, were assembled and were introduced (some for the first time) to a number of local instruments. They were then asked to make a criticism of these instruments and to suggest improvements in them. Their criticisms were numerous: lack of power, rather sours tones, awkward technique made painful to execute through the illogical conception of certain instruments, limited range, absence of semitones, etc. We see here how these Oriental students reacted like a non-specialized Occidental when confronted by « barbaric instruments ». The professors forced them to behave like iconoclasts, causing them to renounce in a few hours the ancient realizations of their culture before they had had the slightest experience in hearing the expressive potentialities of the instruments involved. On the other hand, a few suggestions were made for the « improvement » of these instruments: add keys to the oboe, increase the volume of the resonating box of a xylophones, etc. But all were in agreement to combine local instruments with the Occidental and especially to quadruple or even quintuple each category of instruments. Experiments soon began and demonstrated that, after several months of rehearsals and apprenticeship, it was difficult for the instruments to keep together without written music. Thus they came to realize that any multiplication of instruments precludes improvisation. It was then decided to *write out* the music that was to be played. Music stands were provided, each with its score, and the smallest iota of personal improvisation was abolished. Only an orchestral conductor was lacking, but one was soon added – for elegance – although no one dreamed of following him. The traditional musicians, in spite of their vast experience and superb technique were treated like nonentities by the pretentious young people of the new dominating class. We can observe a similar phenomenon in the Oriental republics of the Soviet Union in the creation of « folkloric orchestras ». We find that these examples reflect a puerile mentality typical of cultural iconoclasm, which is developing just about everywhere in the world. If attitudes vary from country to country, we must nevertheless recognize that the same spirit dominates everywhere. Take, for example, a report from Tunisia made by Salah El Mahdi: « We have almost lost a great number of our ancient modes – through the use of Occidental instruments incapable of producing the quarter-tones of our music. This problem, alas, continually faces Algeria. The Rast mode has become C major, the Bayati – D minor, and the Segah a mode of E. This situation has given rise to a complex among the young, whose musical culture is essentially Occidental; and to such an extent that they have concluded that the music of their country has too many illogical elements. They are astounded that the mode *Fayati* should be called *Hassine* in North Africa and in Maghreb; and that Segah should be called *Boussalek* in the Orient, while the notes are theoretically the same – that is, approximately – as the notes of D minor ».

Another important aspect of the problem is to be found in the conditions under which traditional music and dance are performed. Just as in the case of the popular song in Europe, the use of the microphone has become so widespread that it seems to be indispensable for the out-of-door musical performances. In this way, the entire village profits from the musical echoes of the marriage of one of the inhabitants. It even happens quite frequently that people rent an electronic set-up cheaply for the day, attach a record-player, and there they are! With no problem of arranging for a marriage orchestra to come and of paying them! The dance is also undergoing almost everywhere profound and serious transformations – one might better say distortions – for the very spirit and purpose of the classical dances are placed in question by the use of stage scenery. Until very recently the Royal Khmer Ballet Still performed only at the Royal Palace on an undecorated stage adapted to its artistic demands. The public was placed on three sides of the rectangular space of the stage, which was slightly lower than the audience, thus making easily visible all the movements of the dancers as they moved towards the four cardinal points. Now that the dancers are frequently asked to perform on a modern theatre stage, they must adapt their dances in front of scenery and between the two sides of the stage, directly facing the audience, massed in front of them. This involves for them problems of expression (formerly inexistent when their free mobility was an integral part of this expression) which they compensate for today by using gestures borrowed from Occidental stage movements. This revision of the staging of the traditional khmer dance hits most deeply at its very roots, at its religious and aesthetic raison d'être, at its symbolism and its plasticity.

Little by little some dance episodes of the repertoire are disappearing – episodes which seem « boring » to « modern » spectators, who no longer know the traditional canons; and, in the same way, certain forms of music tend to disappear to the extent that their performance seems very long to listeners who think that they have learned to live at the « industrial rhythm » and who imitate the reactions of Westerners of an extremely relative cultural level, who have probably never heard « Parsifal » or « The Mastersingers ».

But what is more serious is that this evolution brings with it, irremediably, a transformation of the traditional structure of the music. Through the influence of the radios which broadcast Occidental music incessantly, the musicians gradually come to change the tuning of their instruments and it occurs almost unconsciously that in numerous Asian countries the instruments are now tuned on the basis of the Occidental scale. The Asian musics have scales based on degrees which are distinctly different from those of the tempered diatonic scale. But the former are gradually readjusted to the detriment of their meaning and their expressive quality.

It is worth mentioning here, that, contrary to the case of the art of the traditional vocal style, which is at the moment in a state of crisis and lacks great masters and qualified representatives in certain countries, one has been able to observe during the last decades a revived interest in and a very perceptible development of instrumental technique and virtuosity on the part of the performers of traditional music, especially in India and Iran. This is due in great part to the growing interest shown by foreign musicians.

III

MUSICAL REALITY

NATURE OF MUSICAL LANGUAGES

What characterizes a musical language is, above all, a system of references which determines the placing and meaning of the sounds; there is also the style which alters and gives form to the particular meaning of the melodic forms, wheter modal or polyphonic. In addition to this system of references, may be added the construction of scales, the structure of phrases, intonation, ornamentation, the placing of the voice and its implications in terms of precision and character of the intervals, and the timbre of instruments which, taken together, constitute the distinctive character of a musical language. However, it is impossible to notate most of these elements exactly in the rudimentary notation systems which we use. It is for this reason that the use of musical notation has been a disastrous factor in the study of folklore and in ethnomusicology. The enrichment which the different musical systems might contribute to each other is not only a question of eventual superficial borrowings, more or less successful and often more dangerous than useful, but, quite to the contrary, the discovery for ourselves of completely new fields of musical creation and experience. We should choose today between two attitudes: that of apparent disinterest, which will enable us to enrich ourselves while at the same time allowing those cultures which are different form ours to live; or, the attitude of a cultural empire which will devour the world and which will finish by devouring itself after having dried up the sources of its renewal.

We must not forget that a music of the oral tradition, and all music is to a certain degree of oral tradition, can only live if it is understood and practised by the human group to which it belongs. It is a question, actually, of a collective participation in creation – interpretation and style are essential elements of re-creation – which is a continuous process and begins anew each time. The fact that « to create »means in Asia « to improvise » remains rather incomprehensible to the Occidental, particularly because for us the word improvisation has overtones of amateurishness, and, if one applies it to another culture, a rather disdainful connotation. Not for centuries has the European poet improvised on his lyre; today, he publishes his collected works. A sonata, a *lied* are works which have been thought out and rethought as much by the composers as by those who have adapted, arranged or performed them. Books have appeared, analyzing, measure by measure, the musician's intentions and the various means of expressing his intentions. In contrast to this, in Asian music there are no intentions of the author since there is no author, no documents to study and make comments upon, since nothing is notated and the music remains – what it perhaps always should have remained – an ensemble of sounds which evaporate as quickly as they are born but which are, however, always born again. In the European's mind, improvisation seems to be classified as a « primitive » procedure, which he himself has even lost the ability of practising; and, due to this fact, he can only be an inactive witness to the breaking down of the most creative musical cultures as if it were a question of an inevitable evolution.

The principles on which a musical system rest determine the particular characteristics of the form and development. In Occidental music, the timbre of voices, instrumental technique, the melodic or polyphonic conception, the evolution of musical thinking – whether past, present or future – are governed, much more than one is inclined to believe, by the logic of the tempered systems from which we can detach ourselves only with great difficulty, precisely because the timbre of voices, violin technique, the way in which the piano and organ are built lead us back inevitably to that system. We consider moving on from the 12-tone system's semi-tone to the quater-tone – an anti-acoustic conception of the musical scale and unimaginable in the Hindu or Persian systems – because the logic of our theories may lead us to this point eventually. We find Oriental voices ugly and sharp, the bowed instruments scratch, which might be the case if it were a question of our own systems, while from an Oriental point of view, our voices and our instrumental techniques are weak, imprecise, exasperating. The tempered scale, when its tones are pure, is extremely hard for the ear and obliges us to seek a technique of cloudy sound, which, due to our becoming accustomed to it, appears to us as one of the beauties of our vocal art. The vibrato of the voices and of the violin and three strings of the piano, supposedly at a unison but actually creating a harmonic fogginess, soften the sound and blur the precision of the interval, a precision which is essential, incidentally, in modal music of the Hindu or Persian type. It is our being used to these badly-defined sounds which makes it impossible for us to comprehend musical forms in which the intervals are dry and precise. In the Hindu system, the division of the scale is different from our own in its principle. Even when the two seem to be similar, the logic of each leads in different directions. In the Hindu system, all sound relationships are conceived in reference to a fixed tone, the tonic. This creates in the listener an entirely different psychological mechanism, which demands an extremely fine precision in the intervals and, consequently, sharp voices which can differentiate and make use of the very close neighbouring notes, often only a slight fraction distant, but which seem to have an entirely different meaning such as the difference between the soft, tender, passive harmonic third and the more enterprising, militant, bright pythagorian third, for example.

The procedure by which the musician at first identifies himself with the « ground » which is the tonic, and then creates the modal consciousness which enables him to improvise – but which would be lost if he wished to play a fixed melody – is a very special mental mechanism which lends a particular value to the intervals – an expressive value that is unknown in other systems. This expression is further intensified by the fact that the same frequency represents, in the course of a whole piece, the same interval and, when the meaning of a note has been realized, the impression it creates becomes accentuated each time the note is repeated; this sometimes goes so far as to produce an effect of suggestion which can become hypnotic. It is because of the nature of the modal system, conceived as a system of relations to a tonic, that the Hindus divide the octave not into a neutral scale of quarter-tones but in more numerous intervals, cleverly contrasted and very precise, sometimes positive, sometimes negative, which they call *shruti-s* and which constitute a basic division into 22 unequal intervals presenting definite expressive characteristicis and forming a vast vocabulary which, with a little training, one can learn quite quickly to appreciate, for it corresponds to the natural apptitudes of our audio-mental system.

Thus, we can see that there exists an almost absolute interdependence between the nature of the voices, the style, the technique and the musical theory, which makes it necessary to preserve these different elements if we wish to save the whole of the systems. And it is precisely because it is a matter of really different systems that the preservation of the diverse musical languages is so important. The fact that in certain periods certain systems were crystalized or fixed or have been regressive for external reasons, does not at all imply that they cannot again open up possibilities of considerable development. Furthermore, what we call stagnation or regression should not be regarded from the Occidental sense of the terms but as an evolving stage in arts different from our own.

Tradition and evolution

The term « traditional music », which one uses, for want of anything better, for the musics of Asia, implies for us a notion of the survival of worn out and fixed forms.

The musical systems in which improvisation plays an important role are, however, in a constant state of evolution and enjoy a freedom in creating which is impossible in the situation where the musician has behind him the weight of a vast printed literature, which obliges him, in the long run, in order to be original, to turn to the absurd.

The evolution of a traditional art follows its own laws, which only a study in depth enables us to understand. What may appear illogical to us is often in reality a form of the music's vitality. We know that the great art music of a large part of the Oriental countries is, originally and in essence, an intimate art, a sort of chamber music, of a more or less mystical character, addressed to a small circle of listeners. This art is, in its most important and original form, an art of improvisation, and the composer and performer are one and the same person.

Social changes, often nurtured by Occidental ideas, have brought with them a taste for public concerts and the orchestra. This has involved, on the one hand, because of the necessity of playing together, a disdain for or complete abandonment of the principle of improvisation and has, on the other hand, entailed a transformation to increase the sound volume of the instruments so that they can be heard in a larger auditorium. This concern with quantity has led to the introduction of timbres unknown in the past evolution of the art music, has falsified and altered the tonal qualities – vocal as well as instrumental – in the classic tradition; thus this concern has caused the art music to submit to the demands of the orchestra and of the fixed text provided by notation.

Very little place is left for the personal contribution of the musician who is restricted to following a score with his colleagues. The result is a mass of sounds, without personality and totally denatured in relation to the original. But modal music, in general, if it develops, can do so only in its most significant structure (evolution of the scale under external influences, borrowing of instruments from neighbouring cultures, etc.) and then only very slowly. The impelling element of improvisation is always retained.

The musics of highly developed cultures, such as we can hear them today, have arrived at a certain stage in their evolution, and their progress is oriented towards a perfectioning of the art and towards an adaptation within a relatively stabilized society; and this is, furthermore, a sign of vitality. It is in the decadent societies that the arts degenerate and people run after novelty and change.

One should not forget that improvisation provides the special nature of some of the great traditional forms with the indispensible conditions of its life and continuity. Whereas the importance given to quantity, which we have mentioned before, inevitably ends up by a simplification and uniformity which threaten and fix the individuality of the design, of the arabesque, the melodic ornamentation and the rhythmic freedom. These elements, refined and fragile, are not of a secondary importance – as is sometimes the case in Occidental music – but play a fundamental role in the art music of modal type, in which the group of tones which we call an ornament actually stands for a « word » corresponding to a precise meaning, somewhat as a « chord » in harmonic music. No one can say that present-day Javanese music is the same as that performed in the kingdom of the Shailendras, or that Khmer music is still the same as that played in the time of Angkor. A long and slow evolution covers centuries, each pupil learning first the tradition from his masters and later contributing a part of himself to the art – something which has nothing to do with his predecessors. The canons of the art themselves evolve and each musician has his own style. That is why, when we speak of traditional musics, we generally do so in relation to our own tradition of change. This differentiation is doubtless not entirely justified. In any case, when we speak of the systems of traditional music of the Orient, we usually refer to the musical systems based on different principles, different usage of the possibilities available in the relationships of sounds, different scales, timbres, styles, modes and principles of composition other than our own. There remains the task, furthermore, of defining them, for in many of the Asian cultures, music has neither notation nor an established technique for making musical instruments nor analysis following established rules.

If, on the other hand, we observe the new tendencies which have been altering the development of music in Oriental countries, we shall see that the causes have no reference to the aesthetic itself but arise from a psychological crisis, which has led to de-personalization and to de-nationalization, both of which are characteristic of all contemporary art. For the essential aim of the new musics is not the broadening of limited musical concepts to embrace larger and richer forms, but, on the contrary, to limit music to anti-national elements – to anti-individualist, anti-particularist elements. And, if we reflect on the psychological consequences of this tendency, we shall see that it represents in many cases, if not in all, a veritable cultural suicide, in favour of inhuman abstractions. This could be regarded, in the collective consciousness, as a warning omen of a general suicide of what in earlier times was humanism.

The first phenomenon which we observe in the evolution of music in Asian countries is the fear of being « different ». This is linked historically with the political, economic and industrial predominance of the Occident and its religious and cultural imperialism. If you do not dress, speak, eat, drink, think and believe like the Occidentals, you are an inferior, ridiculous, provincial person, in short, a « savage ». This feeling of inferiority extends as well to the whole set of values, customs and morals, even though what is sacrificed represents on certain levels a far more highly developed, more refined and more « modern » form than the Occidental substitute proposed. It is a similar feeling in the Occident which leads to the arrangement of folklore before « serving » it to the public.

The first steps towards this evolution are, at the musical level, purely theoretical and semantic. It suddenly appears absolutely necessary to have orchestras, conductors and composers even in cultures whose musical language consists chiefly of improvised monodic forms. The result is aesthetically absurd and emotionally revolting, but people feel it essential at all costs that the magic terms of the international vocabulary be applicable to the national music, just as today, in the West, certain terms borrowed by musicians from the vocabulary of mathematics or physics are often used against all good sense. The Oriental governments, to this end, give very strict orders to the radio stations, they found Music Schools and create those strange hybrids of orchestral formations, which pretend to use the national music tradition in adapting it to polyphony and try to convince themselves that this is a perfectly natural development corresponding to the unexpressed needs of the contemporary listener. This sort of music, which we can hear in most of the Arab, Indian, Chinese and even Japanese films, does not reveal any of the technical characteristics of Occidental polyphony, but can be described à la rigueur by using the international terminology. It shows no real knowledge, however, of the criteria of polyphony.

We can observe in the Occident today, although we are rarely ready to admit it, that, as in the case of Asia, the evolution of contemporary music is most often not a natural aesthetic evolution. We allow ourselves to be carried away by a sense of a sort of fatality, through a feeling of duty towards the future, by forms of new music which are neither natural to us nor, most often, agreeable, but which we believe to be inevitable, just as the citizens of the socialist countries accept a way of life which, in practice, deprives them often of the pleasure of living; they accept it as the expression of an inevitable evolution towards a future improvement of the human condition.

At the beginning of the 20th century, it seemed necessary to renovate and modify the principles which had served the composers of the preceding centuries. Beginning with Schönberg, who built the twelvetone system, composers further developed it to free themselves from the tempered scale and modality, which had been the basic materials fo all their predecessors.

The public's difficulties in understanding dodecaphonic or serial music came from the difficulties in discarding the notion of tonality, so established in our auditive habits. Few of us dare to admit that after the effort needed to listen to contemporary music – whether abstract or concrete, electronic or mechanical, it is not unpleasant at all to be lulled, while facing the problem of the traffic, by the insipid charms of an Italian or French song, the sort of folklore which represents a pale reflection of 19th century music and which the car's radio serves up to us. The general public, as a whole, remains nostalgically attached to these obsolete forms whose language – poor as it may be – belongs to the romantic age and is no longer considered to be the language of our time.

IV

THE MUSICIANS

THE CONDITION OF THE MUSICIANS

The inferiority complexes of the traditional musicians – which the authorities accentuate by the discrimination which they show against traditional music in general – diminish still more the chances of saving the traditions. Tran Van Khê emphasizes this point:

This inferiority complex continues to exist, and, even now, when a Viet Namian student goes around with a two-stringed fiddle, he tries to hide the instrument, while, on the contrary, when he is carrying a violin, he is very proud of it. This inferiority complex exists because, in the conservatories they do not try to give a favoured place to the teaching of traditional music – in fact, quite the contrary. There is now a sort of entrance examination for the conservatories; those who make good marks are allowed in the piano classes; those with low marks are advised to take up traditional music. This is why, right at the beginning, the music student already has acquired an inferiority complex when he regards the professors, for the professors who teach Occidental music arrive at the Conservatory in a car, while the professors of traditional music arrive by bicycle!

The problems are further complicated by the attitude of the various categories of musicians as they look to their future possibilities. The least one can say is that there is a reciprocal incomprehension between two tendencies: a ferocious, pitiless war goes on between the partisans of the musical language of highly developed art established by a long tradition, who accuse their adversaries of heresy and condemn the sort of education advocated by the « moderns », and, on the other side, the partisans of would be musical innovation who, in their turn, accuse the other side of conservatism and of being opposed to any modernism.

In many cases, only Occidental music is now considered as art music while all the rest – that is to say, traditional music – is relegated to the category of folklore. If one follows this line then one simply allows the musical culture to perish, or one fixes it up to suit the taste of today – that is, one tries to adapt it. To accomplish the latter, one demands that the music change its physiognomy – that it give up its originality to conform to uniform international patterns.

It must, in fact, be recognized that in the industrial civilization customs and traditions tend to disappear to make place for a uniform life which one encounters on all the continents. And the necessity to play – or to listen to – music tends to disappear, especially when music is associated with a way of living or social or religious rites which are no longer practised. In this case, then, how is it that the shadow-theatre could hold its own against the movies and the folk dancer against rock-and-roll? Because, in most cases, either the industrial civilization obliterates the ancient cultures and takes their place or it forces a hybridization which depersonalizes or deforms the survivals of ancient cultures by making them parodies for tourist consumption.

In any case, the music of Asia remains a very particular phenomenon whose problems can in no case be resolved through the concepts or reasoning of Occidentals. In the first place, the musician himself practises his art under very special conditions. This situation varies from country to country in the Orient, but almost everywhere one can say that the traditional musician finds himself in a social situation that is considerably inferior to that of the musician who plays today's Occidental music; and this, incidentally, as a result of a recent evolution.

In India, China and Japan, music is a profession, but in the countries of South-East Asia, professionalism in the Western sense of the term no longer exists today as far as art is concerned. The traditional musician has another occupation, usually farming. If one asks him to take part in a wedding party or a funeral ceremony, he usually does so for a very modest price. Furthermore, music in a village society which finds its raison d'être in day-to-day life, is opposed to the spirit of professionalism as it exists in the Occident. The traditional musician perfects his technique and plays, to be sure, for the pleasure of producing some lovely sounds, but he plays, too, because music is his personal contribution to his religious faith or to the life of the group to which he belongs. He is heard in a closed circuit, so to speak, and his reputation scarcely goes further than his village or his country.

Economically speaking, his art seems less a means of making a profit than a supplementary activity to his work as farmer or artisan. Consequently, when facing the musicians of Western music, he finds himself continually in an inferior position, since those musicians must study a specialized school for the sole purpose of earning their living; whereas the traditional musician learns to play at odd moments and for his own pleasure, the performer in a European type of orchestra « learns » from the start to acquire a metier. These two sorts of musicians consequently differ in the very spirit of their art, beginning with their education. The gap becomes rapidly wider: the one continues to play in his province while the other, as soon as he leaves school, will be appearing in concert halls and radio studios.

Thus, we see that from a material point of view, there is created from the outset a flagrant inequality. It is the same story on the psychological plane: while the traditional musician is heard only by a small circle of listeners, the other is the one who « plays modern music », that is, the one who responds to what is considered locally as the demands of our time. And all this misfortune comes from the generally widespread idea that « modern » music is necessarily music of the Occident. Consequently, the traditional musician remains hidden in his village, and it is with this often disdainful attitude that he is sometimes hired to play in the cities and to provide « local colour » for the tourists. Actually, it is much more a question of ignorance than disdain: the usually modest origins of the traditional musician, whether Occidental or Oriental, often form an insurmountable barrier which prevents him from making himself known. How can a peasant get himself heard if he does not know anyone at the radio or in the specialized institutes or schools? For one is faced with this problem in almost all of the countries of the Orient: the traditions are preserved among the rural populations, not because they are of peasant origin but because the city people have abandoned the traditions. However, these rural populations are not capable, because of their habits and their standard of living, to achieve rapidly an intellectual status which would enable them more easily to make themselves known or to impose their views on an aesthetic basis.

Furthermore, since the cities have adopted Occidental manners and morals, the « milieu » of the traditional musician remains the country, where the rites have been best preserved; there, where he can have constant recourse to the sources of the tradition. The ancient cultures are becoming gradually folklorized.

And still, particularly in the realm of artisanship, certain villages acquire such a reputation that their products are in great demand at a high price. This has occurred in the villages of lace weavers in Laos, of jewellers in Cambodia, whose products are highly prized by local people as well as by foreigners. Examples of this kind are also frequent in Indonesia. Generally, the governments aid such artisanship enterprises since the products become material for exportation.

But for music, up to now, it has not been at all the same. In fact, music, up to a very recent period, did not have any support and traditional music depended essentially on local consumption. But the long-playing record could very easily have changed the situation and given this music the means of having a far wider promotion. There again, Occidental music invaded by means of records the farthest-flung regions, not reached by radios, while no effort was made to find a market which could nevertheless, be very far-reaching for the « artisan » music of the Asian countries.

On the other hand, the conditions of the new ways of life among the young leads to a progressive disinterest of the local public in music.

One can, in fact, make the following observations: it is a universal phenomenon that a child of rural origins who is sent away to school has no desire to « return to the land » later on. Contacts with a certain modernism and a new way of life have rapidly changed his manner of thinking and one can observe a lively, unthinking tendency to abandon his traditions in order to appear up-to-date even in the first years of his studies; he forces himself to be interested in this new hybrid music and ends up by having a taste for it; for one hears it over all the radios, as well as the light music from the Occident, for which he also develops a taste – not from personal preference but because it is fashionable. The young who do not go beyond primary school, who remain in their villages and who, at the same time, hear Occidental music over the radio all day long, remain faithful nevertheless to the music of their country. This simply shows how much the movements of people, contacts with modern civilization, education founded on systems foreign to them, are disastrous for the preservation of cultures. But at the same time one cannot say that the mere listening to light music alone is sufficient to cause the abandonment of traditional music. As we said earlier, a traditional music can only be a living music and it can continue to live only if it participates in the cultural life which serves it as a framework. It is consequently a complex problem since the arts only develop within the context of a particular civilization but today are encouraged only for their international value. Therefore, it is necessary to arrive at a coexistence of culture along with a mutual interest based on a purist appreciation of a work of art and on a rejection of popularizing adaptations. An appreciation of external elements is essential in the modern world, but this appreciation should be illuminated by a genuine artistic education. A recent case in point is the Indian sitar player, Ravi Shankar, who, after having been one of the greatest instrumentalists of India, was severely criticized in his own country for concessions he allowed himself to make before the American public, which indiscriminately acclaimed the perfectly performed rágas no less than the virtuoso exhibition of the soloist, who improvised in the manner of jazz musicians « in the American spirit » and to please a public attracted by circus tricks. Furthermore, a certain public now listens to certain rather fanciful concessions of Ravi Shanker as if these were examples of great Indian music. To confirm this, it is sufficient to look through-and listen to – the long list of records of the great sitarist. However, it is probable that in the long run, with the improvement of the public's taste, such concessions will no longer be necessary or profitable. Ravi Shankar, himself, who is a great classical musician, is now gradually giving up the showy fantasies which were essential to his success.

This problem of preserving a purity of style of some music by individual musicians or groups from the Orient who tour abroad has become painfully worriesome. It is of course understandable that a European public unprepared for Asian cultures cannot at the outset have the same reactions to a concert of Oriental music as the native people. When the musicians note a positive reaction from the public, they are tempted to reproduce the effect which provoked this reaction (often due to the listener's vague reminders of rhythms, timbres or melodic lines to which the public is already accustomed in their own music) and consequently one can understand how the rapid deterioration of the music performed could occur.

The musician becomes little by like an actor who repeats his tricks when he notices that the public reacts favourably. His concerts change, gradually, into a music-hall number from which inspiration is excluded or is transformed into a commercial « method ».

THE PROBLEMS OF INSTRUCTION

The development of a civilization which is essentially concerned with masses tends increasingly to eliminate individual instructions as it always has been conceived in the Asian countries. The techniques of alphabetization, the material needs involved in recruiting the pupils, the selection of teachers, etc. has brought with it everywhere in the world the establishment of collective instruction, based on methods and principles coming from the Occident. But the acquisition of a culture occurs from infancy within the family and thereafter in the village or quarter which represent in themselves the various aspects of the society and culture that have been established through many centuries of traditions. Modern instruction demands that the young move from place to place, demands a new rhythm in work as well as in their way of life – that is, a psychological and social orientation different from what they would have acquired, had they remained in their own milieu.

There is also a disassociation between the customs, social manners, beliefs and rites which form the principal elements of a family education, and a school instruction which does not take these elements into consideration at all or which is even based on contrary principles, which make the subjects of study a world apart, abstract speculation separated from life and incapable of being integrated within it. This explains why Orientals who have been educated in Occidental fashion, are even less capable than foreigners of finding applications of what they have learned to the social, economic or cultural problems of their own country.

Let us look at the case of the training of the young Cambodian. When he was very young he went to the monastery for instruction – the binding force and vital centre of the village. There he learned the prayers taught by the monks, and then how to count, just enough to be able to get along later in ordinary life. In the evenings, the elders came together in the monastery and told each other the legends and historical or mythological fables which were always lively, while in a corner nearby a group of musicians spent the evening playing for them. At the same time, an old sculptor carved the archway of a pagoda depicting some of the heroes of the Ramayana, while telling the people watching him at work the story of their exploits. In these surroundings the young children were freely and quite naturally given the initiative to deveop their own gifts in traditional music, painting or sculpture. At the same time they acquired a great quantity of knowledge as only those who have chiefly their memory for support can impart it.

Thus, from infancy, the Cambodian, living in a closed universe, into which few outside influences penetrated, was brought into contact with the traditional canons which form the basis of his artistic language.

The musical mother tongue had primary importance in the training of the future musician, as important as the spoken language. This training, furthermore, was not based on a logical systemization set up à priori. A Laotian or an Indonesian will not learn the history of his country in the same way as a European pupil, who studies the principal facts of the history of his culture in chronological order. On the contrary, his knowledge is acquired without pre-established order, according to the aptitudes and developing interests of the child and the adolescent. It is not separated from life by that logic which determines that our know-lege be systematically classified, put in definite order, and that each field of knowledge be carefully channelized, separated from the others, in order to be learned later on a global scale. This apprenticeship or rather, this cultural formation, in the Orient, operates much more profoundly, and knowledge is acquired almost unconsciously but with a maximum of participation and of desire to know on the part of the learner. The traditional musician acquires his musical knowledge and ideas in this way. Born amidst a people which plays and knows how to « listen » to music from an angle which is completely its own, he grasps very early the values of his own culture, and when he decides, while still very young, to « make music », he already knows all its rules without having had consciously to learn them systematically. He has then to learn the technique of the instrument he has chosen to play. We see then, that there is no difference really – except for the actual performing – between the musician and the listerner. The latter as well as the former can immediately recognize any piece in the repertoire since he was « born with it ». There is no need, particularly in South-East Asia where music is transmitted orally, to « know » music – with the exception of course of instrumental technique – since it is part and parcel, with no possibility of disassociation, of the cultural frame of reference which includes as well religion, technique or craftsmanship.

Consequently, the contact remains constant between the musician (who is usually also a farmer) and the villagers who know as well as he the pieces of music he plays and who can consequently, pass a judicious judgement on various details of interpretation. In general, one can say that it is the listeners who are the guardians of the real tradition – the tradition in which the musicians of great renown practise their art in their own country. In other words, within a traditional culture, the artists perform what the people uphold and conceive.

This is valid for all the cultures whose main elements are handed down orally. As a whole, the population participates in integrated fashion in the artistic performances of its artists. Actually, it only takes a few minutes to come to know an established canon, a rule of performance (a canon accessible to all), but thereafter the artist must work for months before he can perform the theme perfectly.

In India, the rural population as well as the urban can recognize the rágas or the rhythms, and the most sophisticated performer will find just as attentive and knowledgeable a public in the villages as in the urban centres. This democratic aspect of the traditional cultures in hierarchial societies is a very important factor which should be very carefully studied. It is in the would-be democratic Occident that culture is a question of caste.

In the Asian countries, we are far from that intellectual knowledge of music so extolled in the Occident where art is no longer immediately accessible but has become, in general, the entertainment of a certain category of social classes, who must, in order to understand these arts which have become so foreign to their own cultures, make a special effort to learn about them in order to comprehend them well. We find, however, this participation of the public in certain forms of modern « pop » music.

In most of the Asian countries, the traditional methods of instruction are very similar. Generally speaking, an instrumentalist of repute is surrounded by a circle of young disciples who in the first period listen and « follow » the master through imitation and repetition. An extremely close communion is thus established between the aims of the master and the realizations of the pupil on a spiritual plane at first and, later, on a technical plane as progress is made. In South-East Asia, the master generally teaches a whole piece which the pupil endlessly repeats until he has totally assimilated its musical intentions. He accompanies and aids the master when the latter plays, providing background on the drum or another instrument which he can already play well. At the same time, the disciple absorbs all the culture of his own world, which is inculcated in him without effort by the repeated contacts with the master. Through this procedure, tradition is respected and is enthusiastically pursued. Only personal instruction can enable a student either to become a musician or to be equipped or inclined to listen to and love a form of music that expresses the way of thinking and feeling which is at the core of a particular culture.

In this sort of personal instruction, where the pupil is in regular contact with the master, artistic training precedes the technical. The pupil is in constant contact with the work of art in its most developed form and he is conscious of the goal which he should eventually attain; the content of the music is never separated from its form. There are no « sonatines » or « easy pieces ». He does not learn to « put expression » into a piece mechanically learned. This is why the scholastic methods which people are trying to introduce in the « new » musical instruction succeed in training neither the public nor the artists. Only personal instruction, when the pupil lives with the master, makes possible the true continuity of forms of musical art in which style and expression play a greater role than the form. As in the case of spoken language, which is not learned by beginning with grammatical and versification rules, modal music cannot be studied by beginning with theoretical rules.

It often happens today that representatives of the ancient systems have lost contact with their theories. The instruction they give then becomes purely oral in the literal sense of the word: the pupil listens to and imitates his master. The sources of spontaneous renewal then have a tendency to dry up, great art tends to shrink to folklore, which itself, if sufficiently simplified, loses its character and can be transferred from one system to another, since a simple melody is a common element of all the systems.

In instruction, over-systematic methods freeze the music itself and take away its meaning. W. Malm notes that when he wished to show Occidental students how to play the Javanese gamelan:

The music was based on a fundamental phrase of 16 measures which, according to gamelan tradition, was presented by an ensemble of 4 gongs, a system to which Western musicologists have given the name of coloctonic structure. During my first lessons, I asked the ketuk to play on the odd beats, the kenong to play on 4, 8, 12 and 16, the kempul on 6, 10 and 14, and the gong on 16. The beats were correctly played, but the sense of the structural unity of the piece was weak. At the beginning of a new College year, other students arrived who had heard gamelan music but had never tried to study its structure from a purely intellectual point of view. Before they were « spoiled » by the old students, I tought them to play according to the mnemonic method of « ketuk, pause, ketuk, kenong, ketuk, kempul, ktuk, kenong, ketuk, kempul, ketuk, kenong, ketuk, kempul, ketuk, kenong – gong ». The numbers of the beats were never mentioned, but the new performers got into little trouble since they were helped in the rhythmic structure of the piece by the method they used in learning it. I had the feeling, too, that their performance was more homogeneous than that of the older students, who had learned it with the numerical method.

Traditional music instruction is an integral part of the musical tradition itself and one cannot preserve the tradition without preserving its methods of instruction. Changing the instruction strikes an inexorable blow at the musical structures.

A new type of instruction has appeared in recent years along with the establishment of Conservatories of the Occidental sort, where young musicians learn abstract theories, solfège, and systems of notation instead of participating in a musical experience, a musical creation. They are taught later to judge the music according to purely external criteria and to seek ways of « improving » it. This generally leads them often with the help of third-rate Occidental composers, to want to orchestrate their national music, while they are actually ignorant of its principles. Along these lines, we see musical forms crop up whose idiom is similar to European music of the 19th century, but which uses melodic and rhythmic forms belonging to Oriental traditional music. It is at this stage that the music becomes written music. The works which result resemble arrangements of folklore or the development of folk music themes similar to those which we know in various European countries and especially in Eastern Europe.

The founding of music schools, conservatories, institutes or other specialized units could be effective only to the extent that they were each adapted to the aesthetic demands. The music class as it is conceived today with its professors, its methods and its activity could not in any

*

situation correspond to the needs of an apprenticeship, based on a completely different logic than that which is applied to classical Occidental music. In addition, for each country one must take into account the structure and function of music and create an educational system which fits it. It is, furthermore, less a question of « creating » a pedagogy than it is of using the existing pedagogy within a society that is in the midst of undergoing a transformation. For example, in certain countries of South-East Asia, instruction was carried on in the monasteries. But today it is necessary to go to the school and musical instruction disappears because of this. Consequently, one should create organisms or units in which it would be possible to re-create the material and psychological conditions that the young apprentice formerly found with the monks. In this way, he could learn music and the other arts concurrently with mathematics and other fields so indispensable to contemporary man. Similarly, one should avoid the system of examinations and time schedules for courses and re-establish the relationship of master and pupil in a more human context. This effort was made in the field of the plastic arts around 1910 in Cambodia, and the results were completely positive; one witnessed the resurrection of a dying art and great local artists emerged from this instruction, adapted to the living conditions and customs of the times. An analogous method was very successfully used to save the craftsmanship of Venice.

AUTHORS' RIGHTS

One problem which plays an important role today for the traditional musicians is that of authors' rights. Authors' rights are, in fact, payable only for written music. Consequently, a musician who, through years of hard work, has perfected a form of modal composition and gives a brilliant performance of it is not considered as a composer. But an amateur who transcribes the merest sketch of this performance becomes legally its author. And he will also be able to claim the rights on a gramophone record, while the actual creator has no rights at all.

This priority given to transcription as opposed to creation, from the point of view of rights, creates absurd problems. It is for this reason that some of the great Indian sitar players no longer record the great classical modal themes but are obliged to invent variants which they call new ragas and of which they claim to be the « composer ».

In all music, as a matter of fact, it seems necessary to revaluate the respective roles of the performer and the composer in musical creation.

V

THE FUTURE

The problem of the disappearance of the great systems of non-European music is both a technical and a psychological problem. And it is an urgent problem, because, with a few rare exceptions, the great classical musicians of the Orient no longer train any pupils and the traditional systems which they represent disappear little by little with them. We should perhaps first attack the psychological problem. No music is viable unless it is encouraged and, above all, understood. From the moment that a form of music has an open and understanding public, it can take on importance and the musicians can increase in numbers, for everything, in fact, depends upon the attitude of the musicians themselves who, if they are discouraged, will change their metier or will practise their art only without enthusiasm and let it decline. As soon as sufficient honours will have been given, with discernment, to the representatives of the great systems of pure music and not to the creators of hybrids and substitutes, half the battle will be won.

We should remind the Orientals that to make themselves respected and to maintain their independence, peoples need a currency of exchange and that, on the cultural plane, this currency consists chiefly of the originality of their civilization – and, in particular, of their musical tradition. The Western superiority complex in these matters, which, incidentally, corresponded to a conscious and wilful policy of cultural annexation, often reduced to nothing the efforts of the Oriental countries to have their culture revalorized the whole world. The situation today, however, has changed a little due to the fact that direct relations are occurring more and more between artists, without going through the channels of the governments and the so-called « cultural » propaganda services. In addition, the musicians of the Occident are now less sure of themselves and are eager to broaden their knowledge and deepen their sensibility by familiarizing themselves with different cultures from which they can not only borrow themes and rhythms but above all can acquire new and important conceptions and aesthetic approaches. We should all remember that it is in maintaining the great classical traditions in their most diverse forms that the means of self-renewal will always be nurtured and that change and living creativeness are possible only on a stable foundation and in relation to norms which are handed down to us from the musical experiences of the past. It is only in the last few years that several European musicians, composers or performers, have revealed a more enlightened eclecticism and that they no longer consider, a priori, the Oriental musics as the poor relations of what one might call universal music.

The reaction – conscious or not – of the countries of the Orient to the invasion by Occidental music was intensified by the superiority complex of the Occident which, in a completely natural way, brought not only new techniques but also a manner of thinking which has gradually become imbedded in all of these societies which are in the process of modernization. But, a knowledge of the extra-European arts is becoming more and more indispensable. We discover in them possibilities of enrichment, sources of inspiration which are considerable, although up to now they have been scarcely suspected. We also find in them elements which enable us to understand our own culture better. We should today give aid to the maintenance of forms of art which are part of a vast, common heritage and are not only of touristic interest. We must give back to the countries of the Orient their pride in their national heritage by internationalising it and by putting the music which belongs to their cultural tradition on a plane of equality with Occidental music.

How can one eventually slow down what may seem to be the natural evolution of things. Various means seem possible: the first would be the creation of several serious study centres for comparative musicology, not limited to making collections of recordings or of photographic documents, but extending the work to include the learned theories of the various systems, their conceptions of intervals, of musical relationships, of modes, of development, of composition, of improvisation, of rhythm, of the tuning and manufacture of the instruments, of polyphonic and monodic expression, of style, of vocal technique and, in particular, of the semiology of music – of what a particular system can express or communicate. This would make it possible to provide all of those interested in the problems and possibilities of musical language with a solid and practical and (this time) genuinely scientific documentation, whether they may be in Asia, in Europe or onother continents.

Another means would be to make a very intense effort in all the regions where the great systems of traditional music still survive to maintain with great strictness the purity of the classical art, the ancient methods of instruction, the purity of styles – and thus succeed in abolishing the hybrids.

It seems to be already very late, in certain cases, to correct the regrettable errors that have been committed, and especially in regard to the dramatic issue of hybridization. The public is already accustomed to listening to this sort of music and has come to have a taste for it. In Thailand, for example, every bar now has its classic dance troupe (in the style of the royal dances) and the corresponding type of orchestra. The costumes have been « adapted » to please the tourists and the staging has been done in a way that will not confuse the poor tourist too much. At the end of the dance, the dancers sing out a joyful « byebye » to the balcony. The Thai people, going through the growing pains of modernism, end up by appreciating these dances so admired by the tourists; only a few years ago they would have found them ignoble. It is a sort of sudden jump from ballet at the Opera House to a nightclub show. The technique of the art, however, is not yet lost and it would not be very difficult to re-establish centres of classic art whose production would be worthy to appear before a cultivated public.

One should not forget that in each of the Asian countries there are enormous English, French, American and German cultural centres, with considerable means at their disposal to propagate their national cultures and denationalize the youth of the country. None of these organizations shows an interest in the culture of the country. which has for support only a government, which itself is under constant pressure from the Occidental countries.

What one must particularly oppose is the desire to synthesize fundamentally different arts. We should first of all improve our own education, broaden our musical horizon and encourage in every possible way in the countries which still possess a great musical tradition, the maintenance of this tradition in its purest form with its methods of instruction, its style, its technique, its instruments, its framework and the limited size of its audience. Although one must acknowledge that it would be an extremely difficult undertaking – and all the more so in that the psychology of the masses evolves at the same rate as the progress and increase of modern means. An art can preserve its criteria only if it develops within a given frame of reference. But we are witnessing the total upheaval of cultural values which have been « crushed » by industrial developments. One must facilitate the contacts and trips of artists representing the great systems of music and create a climate of mutual esteem. This is not difficult to do, for we are dealing with admirable things. We must make sure that our best performers play Bach in Teheran and that we hear in Venice or Paris the sublime songs – the immortal works – of Hafiz and of Saadi. It will not be the Oriental Debussys or the Oriental superficialities of our composers which will enrich our heritage or allow us to understand ourselves. We must have the genuine, the authentic – even if, at first, it is difficult. All our efforts to support the maintenance of the great musical traditions will be generously repaid, for they will open up to us spheres of expression and experience whose beauty and richness we can scarcely imagine. To be able to fight against the destructive influence created by the increasing domination of Occidental music over the countries of the Orient and which does not mean for these countries a real participation in Occidental life, but simply in the creation of imitative sub-products, it would be necessary to find the necessary means to counterbalance this badly directed influence. To do this, one would have to use in the most profitable manner the technical media which industrial civilization has put at our disposal.

We have seen that the modern media of dissemination have facilitated the spreading, to a horrifying degree, of Occidental music. It seems therefore certain that a judicial use of these techniques would make it definitely possible, if not to reverse the roles, at least to give back to the musical languages of other cultures their rightful place. Furthermore, the Occident could be more easily receptive to the cultures of the Orient if the more important commercial means were available. With the taste for travelling due to the facilities of communication, the desire to know about something which comes from far away grows. It is enough to see how the art books dealing with the archeology of the countries of Africa, the Orient and the ancient Americas increase by the hundreds and are sold, in order to imagine that it could be the same for the sale of records of extra-European music. This would entail a work in depth which would demand planning, using all the tricks of the trade to mould the tastes of the Occidental listener (conferences, concerts, broadcasts, films, etc.). It is well-known that when a speaker passing through a French city shows and talks about some films he has taken in some far off countries, the record shops are immediately besieged by orders for records of the music of these countries. The problem in Europe is therefore first to create a certain curiosity, then to supply the necessary cultural materials to satisfy it. Only in this way can the interest in the different conceptions of musical art grow.

And in this particular case, the influence of the Occident could become beneficial to the culture of Asia. Actually, when the traditional musicians see their audiences shrinking in their respective countries, the public is really increasing abroad. And it is by following this path that the musical art of Asia could be saved. The Asian countries lay great weight on the opinion of the Occident concerning their own possessions and what they produce. A more marked and informed interest on the part of the Occident in the music of the different countries of Asia would budge the local governments into taking decisions on behalf of the preservation of the authentic musical traditions and dances, for it is the countries themselves which must make, first of all, the first steps.

Many of the national radios have succeeded during the last years in establishing catalogues of taped music, some of them quite extensive. This is certainly a type of useful work which could be easily applied towards the education of the general public – local as well as foreign – to bring about a better appreciation of the diverse musical cultures. But, as we have said above, this solution, while desirable everywhere, is at best a makeshift. It is true, of course, that the art music is partially included here and has its place to the extent that it is based on the very strict rules and is performed by professional musicians. But until now it has often remained in the hands of small, specialized groups or of certain classes of the population. This is true, for example, in the case of sung liturgical music or royal musics, etc. Such forms of music could easily be recorded and even sometimes, broadcast, and they would thus reach a broad representation of the population. But radio broadcasting does not necessarily promote the music if it is not a source of regular employment for the musicians. And this must be sought in the face of the increasing dangers of extinction which threaten traditional musics. Some solutions have been investigated, especially in Japan, where an original one has been initiated: a law was established by the Ministry of National Education to confer an official title on musicians of high accomplishment – a step which has strongly contributed to a recognition of the importance and value of traditional Japanese music. The title given to the musicians thus honoured is « Living National Treasure ». A similar effort has been made in India. It seems that by similar actions, it may be possible, on the one hand, to bring a new consciousness of the beauty of their living art to societies which are moving away more and more from the traditional sphere, and, on the other hand, to interest the public in general and win new adepts.

There remains, however, a great deal to be done to make the governments wake up to the fact that the musical traditions form an integral part of their national heritage. It does not occur to anyone today to allow works of art or historical monuments to fall into ruin through erosion, though we must not forget that in certain countries the preservation of historic monuments is very recent. It was only in the 20th century that a law was made forbidding the destruction of the ancient temples in India – temples, which up to then had served as quarries for the construction of railroad embankments: a typical contribution of a colonizing country and its price. It seems too that other possible solutions could be found to save the musical heritage – beginning with the traditional realities and not at all with the procedures used for Occidental music. Another solution would be to organize numerous competitions, at first national and then international, in which the musicians of all provinces and later of different countries would be invited to come together for the occasions. By this very simple procedure, the possibilities of development would become considerably extended. According to the different circumstances, these competitions could be organized by villages or cities, and the entire population would then quickly take an interest in this kind of undertaking. The success of soccer championships is based on the same spirit of competition.

The fact alone that people come to a village to record music is sufficient sometimes to revive an interest in a large group: it is a universal rule; it is sufficient for the outside world to show an interest to see a flourishing of the artists and of artistic realizations. The problem is only to create an interest in the noble art – and not in a vulgar art.

Once the government shows an interest in the musicians, groups immediately would organize themselves, the instrumentalists would work and the feeling which the musicians have now of being neglected and that their art no longer interests anyone would immediately disappear. In most of the countries, music presents a figure of « poor

relation » among the arts and only a well-adapted nationalism would make it possible to revive the arts of the dance
and music in their purest and highest forms.

NEW INITIATIVES

Only very late in the day have certain countries become
conscious of the quality of their traditional music and their
folk music and have conceded that they form an integral
part of their national heritage. Some of the countries, which
have long been under colonial domination, have retained
a somewhat condescending attitude towards what the Europeans would consider to be folklore. Others have turned
with such a will towards the Occident that their local music has completly disappeared from their preoccupations.

Others, which have a high standard of traditional classical music, whose efforts have concentrated exclusively
on the preservation of only one aspect of this art (the case
of Cambodia, for example, until 1964, with its Royal Ballet), had not realized to what level certain forms of art
considered to be « popular » could also achieve a highly
refined development. And others, finally, although conscious of their country's cultural values, have done nothing
because of the lack of material means.

The very sincere efforts of several Asian governments
to establish music schools and national conservatories in
the hope of preserving their musical heritage have generally
had the opposite effect because the methods of instruction,
the selection of students and the outlets for occupation
offered were badly thought out. And they were, furthermore, often influenced for the worse in doing this by
international « experts ».

The Japanese realized in good time how to control
matters and to stem the flood of mediocrity which was

engulfing all the arts. They saved the Nô, the Gagaku and even the more popular forms of their music, while further developing in admirable fashion their understanding of the music of the Occident. Consequently, it can be seen from this that the task is feasible.

For several years, certain countries have been trying to revive their traditional arts – and principally, their music. This has been particularly true of India, where the great interpreters of classical Indian music have once again enormous audiences and receive high fees. A certain number of State or private conservatories have been created and little by little they have abandoned the teaching methods and notation borrowed from Occidental ideas, whose failure has now become evident. Great institutions, like the one created in Bombay by the Tatas, now plan to pension certain great musicians to enable them to train a number of pupils of their choice. In addition, the enormous success of certain great musicians in Europe and America has been very useful in convincing the governmental authorities that they have in classical Indian music one of the most valuable instruments of cultural propaganda, and this has stimulated a renewal of interest for the maintenance of the true Indian musical culture. But it has, unfortunately, not yet been achieved in the other countries of the Orient.

An experiment which has been tried in many place has been the creation of professional troupes of musicians and dancers. Encouraged by the example of already existing classical dance groups, the governments thought that the founding of professional traditional orchestras would be an effective way of keeping alive the different aspects of the national heritage. Without wishing to belittle the merits of such a plan of action, one must nevertheless confess that this solution is not satisfactory. In fact, the Asian classical dance troupes are part of an organized not be able to continue and could not form part of the royal Ballet of Cambodia belongs to the ceremonial « necessities » maintained at the Royal Palace and, at the same time, serves as entertainment for the kings. The Royal Ballet, without a permanently constituted troupe, would not be able to continue and could not form part of the roayl rituals. The case is the same for certain Indonesian groups which belong to the princely courts. Furthermore, the classical dance is based on rigorous ensemble rules which demand continual rehearsals by the whole troupe.

It is clear, then, that the Royal Ballet can only be professional. But for the music or dance in which mime or improvisation hold an important place, it would seem difficult to create professional troupes which would have the responsibility of preserving the most beautiful examples of the art in their original form, outside their habitual public. Traditional art is a sort of sound or choreographic construction which represents a certain vision of life and which can be undertaken only by those persons themselves who feel genuinely concerned by the music. The art of a traditional civilization remains in Asia something profoundly alive, something profoundly active and dynamic, which has extremely little to do with the pale musical remains which one can still find in certain rare provinces of France or Italy, remains of ancient cultures – obsolete today – and of which there survives, by chance, only a lullaby or a work-song which some old peasant still hums, without great conviction.

In reality, the musical art of a traditional civilization expresses itself in many different facets; these fit into a social context in which each piece of music – even if it is sung by the whole population – finds its own special interpreters (recognized by this population), who achieve in their performance the perfection demanded by regional criteria.

In other words, one should not think that an art in which the majority of the population participates and which is sometimes described as popular or « folkloric », is not a professional art, even though it does not exist necessarily by the intermediary of mobile professional troupes; these would be unfamiliar with the *raisons d'être* of its technique.

CO-EXISTANCE OF CULTURES

The defeatism, which makes people think that it is impossible to fight against the standardized cultural products imported by the industrial civilization to which all the Asian countries are becoming adapted, is without foundation. Different cultures can live side by side without imposing on each other their rules and without one of them wishing to appropriate certain aspects of the other. The development of modern techniques is in no way linked to a particular culture. It is solely the commercial power of the over-developed countries which undermines the cultures of the economically weaker countries. It is not the artistic value which is at stake here but purely the productivity, in terms of surplus of cheap records, of grants given by the rich countries to their second-rate artists to use them as propaganda products abroad.

In India the system of castes had been developed to enable very different peoples and civilizations to live harmoniously together without any of the groups imposing its beliefs, its customs or its arts on the other. Similarly, we find in India the most diverse musical systems which co-exist without mixing or harming each other. For centuries, in most of the South-East Asian countries, the populations have been living in close contact with large Chinese minorities, whose place in the social scheme is important particularly in commerce and the technical metiers.

The homes of the different groups are side by side and

the population as a whole participates integrally in the life of the country in which they live. The Chinese minorities, often very numerous and very strong economically, have their own customs, their own music. But the hybridization of Indonesian, Burmese, Laotian or Cambodian music with the Chinese has always been extremely limited if not non-existent. The reason for this is that the cultures, Chinese and local, facing each other, are, on the one hand, functions of beliefs and ways of living and, on the other hand, the power of their means of propagation is limited and identical: the religious ceremonies and the popular celebrations. Thus, these two cultures are neighbouring without in any way mixing or acculturating each other, without one trying to replace the other. The influences of one music on the other are consequently very weak. At most, one can observe the borrowing of instruments or a minimum of technical, instrumental elements, which have not occurred with brutal abruptness but in the course of long periods which extend sometimes over several centuries.

But what is worrying is that the contact with the different kinds of music produced by the Occident provokes in the music of the other civilizations a rapid and doubtless irreparable deteriorization. This is due to the enormous differences in the means of propagation put at their disposal. While the traditional music remains, as we have said above, in a narrow regional framework in the form of living performances, we see an invasion of « canned » Western music take place, which invades and submerges the whole world – thanks to the means of exceptional power exemplified by records and the radio.

The means at play are too unequal for traditional music not to suffer from the repercussions.

Many people consider that this phenomenon is irreversible, that traditional art is condemned and that all one can do is to record what still exists. It goes without saying that this attitude is extremely prejudicial to any revalorization of the traditional musical art. Many musicologists, when they are sure of possessing on magnetic tapes some characteristic examples of a certain kind of music, think that they have done the essential. They are tempted to confuse « put up in cans » and safeguard.

For, in the case of forms of music which are orally transmitted, a recording can only be the image of a given musical moment and could not be considered as representing a synthesis of the music. Recordings should be regarded as piously preserved examples of fragments of a culture, but in no case as a means of protecting musical tradition.

This is the crucial problem with which we are faced, for the Occident could play a great role in the promotion of the musics of Asia if the well-informed public could go beyond this basic incomprehension which is still shown much too often. This is why the Occidental public should be invited to develop more deeply a true knowledge of the Orient instead of reacting to sudden « revelations » of certain forms of music of the Orient. A few years ago, Europe had the « revelation » of Indian music, and now, recently, the « revelation » of Japanese theatre and music. It would be more valuable if a certain basis of these cultures were first inculcated gradually by the radio, records and books. It is always dangerous – considering the facility with which the public sometimes becomes enthusiastic about new ideas – to present Oriental artists, who will certainly have the success which they deserve but not necessarily with much discernment. Too often, a certain public shows its fascination for a musician or a piece of music « because it's Indian » and not necessarily because it is the best of Indian art.

A systematic programme of education needs to be undertaken in the Occident, a cultural « open door » policy which is not only concerned with external forms. If there is an exhibit of Chinese or Egyptian art in Paris, the visitors flock to it. If the Peking Opera or the Royal Khmer Ballet arrives, the theatres are sold out. But these are very passing events, without a spirit of continuity and what is particularly important – without a penetration into the inner meaning of the arts. What is needed is a combination of educational and cultural media: lectures, radio broadcasts, books and records; without these supplementary aids, a concert or a ballet remains a fleeting experience and feeling without a future.

In secondary school, pupils spend six years studying the history of Europe. The ancient or traditional civilizations are passed over cursorily in a few pages. But, today, it takes no longer to fly to Peking than it does to go to Sicily by train – which places Asia actually at our doorstep. The technical media of today should feed our curiosity and enable us to become acquainted with the chefs-d'oeuvres of countries which yesterday were still far distant, and only with export products adapted to our use. One would need to put into motion a complete revision of the artistic education of the European as well as of the Asian. We can no longer continue to be ignorant of the fact that the art of music does not begin with the Renaissance and that many centuries earlier other musics, representing a highly refined art, existed in all parts of the world. Today, still, certain countries like Indonesia « live » intensely and at the highest level a musical art which is entirely different from that of India or of Europe. Too many histories of music have restricted themselves up to now to a limited geographic area, not going beyond the cultural frontiers of a particular civilization. In the European nomenclature, the « musicologists » are concerned only with Occidental music. The great musical cultures of Asia are relegated to the « ethnomusicologists » and are confused with folklore. In the definition which he gives of ethnomusicology in an important Italian encyclopedia of music, Marius Schneider describes it as « the study of Occidental folklore and of non-European musics ».

In the very numerous books on Oriental art and archeology which have appeared in the last years, there has been a genuine opening-up of knowledge about Asia in certain fields. As far as music is concerned, records are also more numerous but their sale, due to the high prices, is still rather weak. Radio broadcasts give a very small place to the non-European musics. As for books, the chapters concerning any music cultures other than the Occidental (when there are any at all) are thin and limited. Monographs find little commercial distribution. Books of popularisation are also extremely rare.

RECORDS

Excellent records are published in some Oriental countries, but they are rarely exported and in no case can they compete with the foreign market. Published in very limited numbers, they are sold locally to replace the orchestras in local ceremonies. The matrices are usually destroyed immediately. No significant effort at distribution in the Occident has been undertaken, for one thing because of the absence of commercial representation abroad, and for another because the quality of presentation (covers and texts) and of pressing is not always of high enough standard in comparison with the quality demanded by the European market. This is understandable in view of the meagre means of the small record publishing houses. Only India and Japan have a large record production of highest technical quality, but no serious attempt has been made to export the records.

Furthermore, the record publishing houses have quickly learned that it is to their interest to bring out « arranged » music or hybrid music. They profit on the commercial level, but the harmful effect is obvious. In Cambodia, the sale of records doubles every year and it is very probably the same story in the other countries of South-East Asia. All of this has very important repercussions on the musical life of the countries. The musical mixtures, spread about by the radio and on records, result in the development of a hybrid music which they call « renovated music ». The same is true in Thailand and in the Philippines, where hybridization is still more pervasive.

THE RADIOS

To oppose this constant predominance of a certain form of Occidentalism, there might still be the radio, which is in principle independent and national, if only one knew how to make good use of it. And there too, in fact, we run into the urgent feeling that they must do something on an equal plane with the Occident and consequently they model their radio broadcasts on the programmes and methods perfected by the European countries. Foreign experts foster, in actual fact, the consumption of Occidental musical goods, if for no other reason than the fact that the recorded tapes arrive ready to be used. Thus, the task of advising, which ideally would consist in helping the directors of the national radios to bring out the values of their own musical heritage, is in reality still another encroachment on the part of the Occident.

It should be recognized, on the other hand, that certain radios have recognized the danger threatening the national culture and have undertaken to develop to a maximum the broadcasts of traditional music, for this policy comes within the plan of maintaining nationalism. More than half of the music programmes in Cambodia, for example, are devoted today to traditional music. In Hong Kong, this same attitude has revived the public taste for Cantonese opera. In Indonesia, the radio is in close contact with the institutes of traditional music and the latter are regularly requested for recordings at the time of annual popular celebrations.

In addition, many radios have their particular artists. This is true in Laos, where the instrumentalists of art music form a group attached to the radio studios. But, on the whole, such arrangements are isolated exceptions and do not form a part of the general planning. In Laos itself, the radio has its own orchestra of Occidental instruments, which plays light music, but also — and this is more serious — « arrangements » of local music. No one would dream of protesting the presence of an Occidental orchestra at the radio. But this simple fact — which seems perfectly natural to everyone — would appear much more bizarre if it were presented the other way round: does the French Radio-Television have its Laotian orchestra? This question, which may cause a smile, actually states the whole problem: this predominance of broadcasts of Occidental origin represents a constant rape of the local cultures of Asia. We should point out too that the broadcasts of light or symphonic music are very smooth and expert in their presentation, with experienced announcers, whereas the « local » musical art must be satisfied with a presentation in a few words, since the authorities always figure — and very falsely too — that these broadcasts are listened to only by the backward elements of the population. In actual fact, a very numerous public listens to the traditional music, both within the country and outside, and a great many would listen more if the presentation of the music were more carefully made. One is consequently forced to conclude that this wonderful medium of radio tends towards a negation of the hierarchy of values, when the most beautiful creations of art music are placed on the same level as the most banal of light music. For it is a fact that all distinctions disappear in the flood of sounds poured forth by the radio, and the radio authorities, generally deformed by a badly assimilated foreign training, rather often regard the listeners who are faithful to their heritage with a certain disdain.

Naturally, any country needs today, in order to survive, to reach the technical level of other countries. From this arises the necessity of developing a modern method of instruction, and of becoming equipped to meet the competition, etc. This forms a break in continuity, all the more serious in that it is rapid and leaves no possibility for a natural evolution. Many countries have jumped from a rural farming life to the industrial 20th century in twenty years, which obviously could not take place without deep psychological upheavals and which leaves them open to all sorts of external influences. It is in this way that « pop » and light music in general, which have invaded the radios of all countries, imbed themselves without difficulty in the most developed levels of society to the extent that most of the young, who are often iconoclasts, and all the more avid since a certain propaganda influences them to believe in the superiority of the way of life and the values of the Occident, renounce today their own cultures. And this is true in many countries.

One cannot struggle in the modern world against techniques. But one must know how to use them to oppose a destructive invasion by forms of Occidental music which are already often demoded in Europe and which could never replace the creative, local art. The material means operating now in this struggle are still unequal. Recordings by jazz groups are brought out daily by the millions all over the world, and one can find in the French record catalogues twenty-five different interpretations of the Pastoral Symphony and forty of the Kleine Nachtmusik. But, in the face of this extension of a market which is spreading all over the world, the quantity of recordings of Indian, Iranian, Indonesian or Japanese music, in competition, is extremely slight. Some countries of the Orient are represented by a dozen or so records of value (published in Europe or in the countries of origin); this is true for Japan; but musical cultures as important as those of Indonesia (with a population of 100 million) or Cambodia are summed up on three or four records which are difficult to obtain. The disparity between the various means available is fantastic if one remembers that three quarters of the population of the globe belong to extra-European cultures.

In the years to come, music festivals will doubtless play an important role in the dissemination of Oriental music. Already now, numerous festivals include in their programmes at least one Asian ballet troupe or group of musicians every year. The festival of the Théâtre des Nations has been for a long time an event in which all facets of contemporary musical and dramatic art were represented, and the list of Oriental groups who came especially to this occasion is already a long one. Other festivals have followed this model and it has now become an accepted custom that during the period of festivals several groups of artists coming from India or elsewhere, make the tour of the various important festival centres. Considering the success of these groups, the movement is growing and will doubtless reach a point where certain festivals will be able to specialize in the presentation of non-European music. It seems as if the present period of transition fosters – especially among the young – this participation or interest in everything that is truly alive. The effect of novelty which all this musical world has for the West goes along with the search for new harmonies and rhythms which preoccupies certain « pop » music of today. There is surely a public ripe now to appreciate this important heritage embodied by Asian art.

The international organizations and governments have an essential role to play in the preservation of the threatened cultures and monuments. There would be very few ancient monuments still standing if the « Fine Arts » did not intervene to prevent their destruction. For the living monuments, which the craft and musical traditions actually are, criteria and methods need still to be defined.

For the countries of the Orient, the international organizations are in many cases paralyzed by the fact that the representatives of the countries concerned are most often entirely oriented towards an extreme Occidentalisation and are totally ignorant of the cultural values of their own countries. Those who, themselves, deplore the loss of the ancient traditions and arts fear being misunderstood and appearing to oppose « development » in their country. This is why they often prefer to remain silent.

If one reads almost any of the questionnaires that Unesco and the other international organizations, interested in a mutual appreciation of different cultures, sent to Asia a few years ago, asking for information about the orchestras, the conductors, the composers, modern works, concert halls, etc., one would understand that the blank places must have been filled in with fictitious information in order not to leave the page completely white.

For several years now, however, Unesco has become aware of the problem. The International Music Council (I.M.C.) collaborates closely today with the International Institute for Comparative Music Studies and Documentation (I.I.C.M.S.D.) whose purpose is to foster the acquisition of a more comprehensive knowledge of the musical art of the civilizations of Asia and Africa and to assure their integration in the field of general culture. The I.M.C. has now formed national music committees in numerous countries of Asia and Africa, in which the most qualified representatives of the local musical systems should, according to their statutes, be members.

Through the intermediary of the Groupe Interculturel d'Information et de Coordination pour les Spectacles et les Concerts, which brings together the directors of the principal festivals, the I.I.C.M.S.D. and the I.M.C. aid and encourage the organization of European tours of great artists from Asia and Africa. They collaborate too with the American Society for Eastern Arts, an American organization with similar aims.

The I.I.C.M.S.D. edits for Unesco anthologies of records of the Orient and of Africa and is preparing a universal history of music on records to make known the chefs-d'oeuvre of the musical art of the various Asian and African civilizations.

The means at the disposal of these organizations, however, remains distinctly insufficient and Unesco and the foundations must be made aware of the urgency of the problems.

The decadence of the non-European cultures has occurred uniquely as a result of the prejudices of the Occident towards these cultures. It is, therefore, by a reversal of this attitude, in giving the place they deserve in the musical life of the world to the great artists of Africa and Asia, that one will cause the disappearance in these countries of their inferiority complexes and will bring about a positive action by the governments to save and give an honoured place to these musical languages which are of inestimable value to universal culture.

In this connection, let us quote Tran Van Khê: « When an international organization invites a traditional musician to perform, it is of great benefit to the culture of his country — much more than through many conferences, because the very fact of inviting a traditional master of authentic music to come to play in Europe, carries with it the mark of highest approval.

... I should like to suggest two things: the first, that as much as possible, in future festivals of congresses, we invite masters of traditional music, even if they do not speak foreign languages; we must consider that in inviting a tradional master we do so not only for himself but also for the tradition itself-a sort of international consecration.

... Mr. Daniélou has done much for traditional music in general since, little by little, in Viet Nam alone, in Saigon, when the young people learned that I could play Vietnamese music in various Occidental countries, that the Musicological Institute in Paris approved the offering of instruction on the Vietnamese cithare in our Centre of Studies of Oriental Music, the young of Saigon asked each other why – if playing the Vietnamese cithare is taught in Paris and they have the possibility of learning to play it at home – they do not do it. And we have noticed that the number of students in Saigon who have requested admission in the cithare class has more than doubled in two years and now, even at the University, the students who study the Sciences and Literature no longer disdain playing the monocord or the two– stringed fiddle.

Several series of congresses, symposia and round tables organized by the I.M.C. and the I.I.C.M.S.D., with assistance from Unesco and the national committees of various countries of Asia, Europe and America, have made it possible over the last ten years or so to pin down more precisely the social, cultural, psychological and technical problems which are at the bottom of the rapid disappearance of the great musical cultures. The documentation we have used for the present study has been almost entirely borrowed from the material of these congresses and meetings. Culture will not survive in any country without considerable effort being made to support education, the preservation of monuments and the cultural heritage, and the encouragement of creative artists. The fact that such efforts have been made for almost two centuries on a musical basis uniquely in favour of Occidental culture explains clearly the decadence of the other cultures. This is apparently the only problem and it should not be impossible to remedy it. The study of the problems which concern the relationships between the various civilizations from the musical standpoint are of fundamental interest because in no other field can we analyze with as much precision the fundamental problems which relate to the coexistence of peoples and cultures. What we may discover in the field of music is immediately applicable to the other fields of life and of the civilization.

We shall be able to find solutions to the fundamental problems created in the colonial era and accentuated by the economic under-development of certain countries which mostly resulted from that period, only if we understand the profound nature of the malaise which resulted and find practical and effective solutions to restore a genuine equality of peoples and races which does not consist of requiring the same behaviour for all but of giving each the right to be what he is as an individual and as a collective group, representing thousands of years of efforts to perfect a civilization, a culture, a language, and refined forms of art.

It is in this fluid and living medium of music that we shall be able to judge the sincerity of the efforts, the true respect of peoples and civilizations towards each other. It is probably not exaggerated to say that the future of the world will depend to a not negligible degree upon what we shall be able to do in the apparently anodyne field of the art of music to enable the various civilizations to flourish again and to know each other better without absorbing each other.

INDEX

368 7 2824